Class 50

The distinctive 'dubbing' sound of a Class 50 on Class 1 main line traffic is now almost a thing of the past. In happier days when the Class 50s were still in charge of London-West of England services, No. 50020 *Revenge* nears Ivybridge with a Paddington-Plymouth relief.
CJM

To many Class 50 enthusiasts the Network SouthEast (NSE) livery applied to over half the Class 50 fleet was rather gawdy. However, it has enhanced the previous relatively dull railway scene with a little colour! On 4th June 1987, No. 50034 *Furious* passes through the Thames Valley at Lower Basildon with the 06.45 Milford Haven-Old Oak Common vans. *CJM*

Life & Times Series

Class 50

Colin J. Marsden

Oxford Publishing Co.

Introduction

Enthusiasm for 'Modern Traction' classes has grown considerably over recent years – the first class to attract an almost cult following was the 'Western' Class 52s in the mid-1970s. This was followed by literally thousands of enthusiasts chasing almost every move of the 22 strong 'Deltic' fleet. Considerable following also surrounded, but on a lesser scale, the demise of the Class 40 and 'Peak' fleets.

Today it is somewhat surprising to record the huge following for the English Electric built Class 50s, as many of the enthusiasts are the same people who, in the mid '70s despised even the sight of a Class 50, because they were ousting their beloved 'Westerns'. This demonstrates how railway enthusiasm has changed over the years. The 'Life and Times of the Class 50s' have, to say the least, been interesting, with the 50 strong fleet built and indeed owned by the English Electric Company, for several years working London Midland Region Anglo-Scottish and Northern Division West Coast Main Line services. After WCML electrification, the 50s were redeployed onto the Western Region, being allocated to Bristol Bath Road, Plymouth Laira and Old Oak Common in London. When first on the WR, after training was complete, the class ousted the diesel-hydraulic Class 52s from their remaining duties, and along with Class 47s and High Speed Trains (HST) formed the backbone of 1980's WR motive power. After only a very short period on the Western the performance of the class became very poor with, on some occasions, insufficient locomotives available to cover the diagrams. This position was considerably improved in the early 1980s by complete refurbishment, a subject well covered in this book. This work eliminated most of the 'As built' sophisticated electronics which were by this time not used, and the cause of many problems.

By the early 1980s as well as operating on the WR, the class were deployed on the Waterloo-Exeter line to replace the lower powered Class 33s, a route on which the Class 50s have performed well.

The demise of the Class 50s commenced in February 1987 with the withdrawal of No. 50011, and by the time the manuscript for this book was prepared almost half the fleet had been withdrawn. Much speculation surrounds the final demise of the fleet, but the author would be very surprised if some examples were not still in traffic in 1992.

With the considerable following that now surrounds modern traction preservation, it is almost assured that at least one member of this much-followed class will be saved, whether or not it will be allowed to operate on the main-line is of course a subject for much discussion.

Although a number of books have been written on the Class 50s, it is hoped that readers of *Life & Times of the Class 50s* will enjoy browsing through its pages, and viewing the Class 50 fleet at work and rest. On a personal note the production of this title has been a most pleasurable task and I should like to thank the many people who have assisted with information and illustrations for inclusion, and especially to Michael Collins, John Faulkner and Michael Oakley for the preparation of complete chapters, and Graham Fenn for providing the line drawings.

Colin J. Marsden
Dawlish, Devon

A FOULIS-OPC Railway Book

© 1991 C.J. Marsden & Haynes Publishing Group

British Library Cataloguing in Publication Data

Marsden, C. J. (Colin J.)
Class 50.
I. Great Britain. Railway services: British Rail.
Class 50 diesel-electric locomotives, history
I. Title II. Series
625.26620941
ISBN 0-86093-420-9

Library of Congress catalog card number
90-84486

Published by:
Haynes Publishing Group
Sparkford, Near Yeovil, Somerset. BA22 7JJ

Haynes Publications Inc.
861 Lawrence Drive, Newbury Park, California 91320, USA.

Printed by: J.H. Haynes & Co. Ltd

Title page photograph: In the view of the author, one of the most pleasant illustrations of the railway at Dawlish is from between the tunnels at Shell Cove. Green-liveried No. 50007 *Sir Edward Elgar* pulls out of Clerk's Tunnel on 25th April 1988 with the 12.03 Portsmouth Harbour-Plymouth service. Dawlish station and town can be seen in the right distance. *CJM*

Contents

The Class 50 Prototype – DP2   7

Design and Construction   10

Technical Description   16

Cab Layout   17

Fleet List   18

In Detail   20

Drawings   21

Performance – The Last Search for Identity   24

The Refurbishing Programme   33

Operations   39

Maintenance   46

Class 50 Names   52

Liveries   55

In Traffic   59

The splendid scenery of the Berks & Hants route between Reading and Westbury, especially along the banks of the Kennet & Avon Canal, has provided photographers with some interesting viewpoints. NSE liveried No. 50023 *Howe* heads a rake of BR blue/grey and InterCity stock near Midgham on 19th March 1987 with the 11.45 Paddington-Penzance.   *CJM*

'Deltic' "look-a-like" English Electric prototype No. DP2, the forerunner to the Class 50, storms north through Hadley Wood in the summer of 1963 with the Saturday Only 10.10 King's Cross-Edinburgh.
A. Natchpole

From its introduction until June 1963, DP2 was deployed on the West Coast Main Line (WCML), where it was used on Liverpool, Crewe and Blackpool services and is seen here in its distinctive all-over Brunswick green livery.
GEC Traction

The Class 50 Prototype – DP2

Following the full introduction of the modernisation scheme diesel classes by the early 1960s, the Railway Board began the search in 1962/63 for suitable second generation main line Type 4 locomotives. These would have the ability to operate at speeds up to 100mph, a feat which was not available with the existing fleets. After BR's interest in 'new' motive power, the three major private locomotive builders all set about designing and building a possible 'prototype' Co-Co Type 4. This led to three highly successful locomotives being introduced, namely from Brush No. D0280 *Falcon*, from a BRCW/Sulzer/AEI partnership No. D0260 *Lion* and finally the subject of this feature, the English Electric 'prototype' No. DP2, the forerunner of the Class 50 fleet.

After the decision was taken that English Electric would produce a prototype, the EE subsidiary of Vulcan Foundry were sub-contracted to effect construction – which utilized a production 'Deltic' bodyshell. The internal layout of the 'prototype' christened from its conception Diesel Prototype 2 (DP2) was, from the No. 1 end: cab vestibule, cooler group, power unit, steam heating boiler and electrical control/power cubicles. The nose end sections housed, at the No. 1 end: two Reavell FRU series vacuum exhausters and the No. 1 end traction motor blower, while the No. 2 nose end accommodated the No. 2 end traction motor blower and the air compressor. The driving cab layout was arranged in the standard English Electric style with driving position to the left and assistant's seat to the right. The rear of the cab housed electrical equipment in two cubicles. The cooler group, supplied by Serck, consisted of a centrally mounted roof fan driven mechanically by the power-unit through an electro-magnetic coupling. The speed of the fan was controlled by a thermo-electric system, which also operated the louvred positions on either side of the locomotive. The cooler section on DP2 was like a separate room with hinged and sliding doors. The central section of the body accommodated the EE16CSVT power unit with its associated EE generator group. DP2 was the first locomotive to use the 16CSVT unit, which was a direct-injection, pressure-charged, inter-cooled V form unit, operating normally at 850rpm. Four Napier pressure-chargers, two on each cylinder bank, were fitted, which were exhaust gas-turbine units.

To provide power for traction and auxiliaries, an English Electric generator group was coupled to the power unit flange. Comprised of an EE840/1B main generator (for traction current), this was a 12-pole unit with a continuous rating of 66kW, 600amp, 110v at 850rpm. The overhung auxiliary generator (for locomotive auxiliary circuits) was of type EE911/SC which was a self-ventilated unit. Moving along the engine from the generator group there was the steam heating boiler, of the Clayton type, able to deliver 2,000lb of steam per hour.

Electric power produced by the main generator was passed to six EE538A traction motors, one powering each axle. The traction motors were 4-pole dc series wound machines rated at 400hp, 533 amp, 600v and were axle hung, nose-suspended units. Traction motor positioning was to the rear of the axle for the leading pair, and to the front for the inner axle, the drive gear ratio being 53:18.

The bogies fitted under DP2 were of standard English Electric Co-Co design and incorporated roller-bearing suspension. The power circuitry was such arranged to fully inter-connect between the bogies and provide three series pairs wired in parallel across the generator. Between-bogie equipment consisted of fuel tanks with a total capacity of 900 gallons.

DP2 was constructed during the autumn of 1961 and was completed in April 1962, from when it was the subject of extensive 'on works' testing. DP2 ventured onto the main line for the first time on 2nd May 1962 when it successfully operated light from Vulcan Foundry to Chester and return. After re-entry into Vulcan Foundry several small adjustments were carried out and a final inspection made by BR prior to acceptance onto BR lines for active service. On 8th May 1962 DP2 was used to haul a 15-coach train of 475 tons between Crewe and Penrith, this outing of 123 miles culminated in the train reaching the summit of Shap at 43 mph.

On 11th May 1962 DP2 was allocated to driver training duties and used for several days between Crewe and Birmingham. This was followed by the permanent allocation to Camden shed from 14th May. During the following months DP2 was regularly used on the following duty:

Monday-Saturday
07.45 Euston-Liverpool (08.15 Sats)
14.05 Liverpool-Euston
19.15 Euston-Perth (to Crewe)
00.30 Crewe-Euston

The deployment on this diagram gave a daily mileage of 704 miles.

At this time DP2 was not diagrammed for Sunday working, this day being utilized for maintenance purposes. By the commencement of the 1962-63 winter timetable DP2 was allocated to the Euston-Carlisle route, where the weekly mileage was approximately 3,800 miles. The main duties over this route involved:

01.25 Euston-Carlisle
13.25 Carlisle-Euston

Again Sundays were kept as spare for maintenance and special duties.

By May 1963 DP2 was estimated to have clocked up some 130,000 miles and was redeployed on the Euston-Blackpool route operating the following duty:

Monday-Saturday
17.05 Euston-Blackpool
08.00 Blackpool-Euston

On a Sunday DP2 operated the 08.05 Blackpool-Euston service then received maintenance until rostered for the Monday 17.05 Euston departure.

Such was the success of DP2 that by June 1963 the English Electric Board, in collaboration with BR, decided that constant supervision by EE engineers was no longer required. This decision was made because the availability to date was almost 100% with only two on-line failures being recorded – one due to adverse weather which froze the radiator elements and one flashover – both faults were rectified the same day.

On 16th June 1963, after some 164,580 miles had been completed, DP2 was returned to its builder's works for bogie attention which included tyre-turning and a 5,000 hr engine examination, which showed the power unit to be in excellent condition. Whilst at Vulcan all electrical equipment was inspected and cleaned and a replacement train heating boiler of the Clayton Type R2500 Mk2, able to deliver 2,500 lb of steam per hour fitted.

In June/July 1963 the English Electric Company approached BR with the view of changing DP2's work cycle and by the end of July the locomotive was transferred to the Eastern Region at Finsbury Park where, after staff familiarisation, the locomotive was placed in the 'Deltic' pool. This was considered by many at the time to be far too taxing duties for a mere 2,700hp Type 4 locomotive on diagrams which required long periods of fast running.

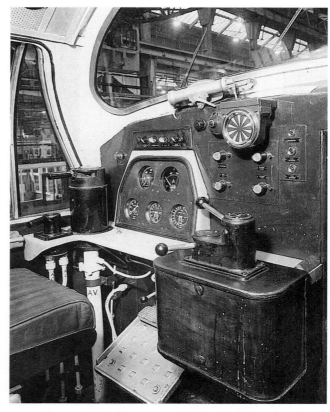

The cab layout used on the DP2 prototype conformed to the company's previous 'Deltic' and BR Type 3 (later Class 37) style. Brake controllers were on the left of the driving position, while the master switch and power controller were to the right, all other essential controls and indicators being conveniently positioned.
CJM

The DP2 prototype was the first EE product to use the 16CSVT prime-mover, a direct injection, pressure charged inter-cooled 'V' unit. This photograph shows the unit prior to installation, with the EE generator group coupled at the far end.
GEC Traction

DP2's debut on ER metals came on 13th July when it operated a King's Cross-Leeds return service, but proper diagramming commenced two days later when its regular duty became:

Mondays
00.46 Newcastle-King's Cross
10.10 King's Cross-Edinburgh
22.30 Edinburgh-King's Cross

Tuesdays-Fridays
10.10 King's Cross-Edinburgh
22.30 Edinburgh-King's Cross

Saturdays
10.10 King's Cross-Edinburgh
20.05 Edinburgh-King's Cross

Sundays
Finsbury Park Maintenance (08.30-15.30)
17.10 Kings Cross-Newcastle

Whilst on this duty DP2 achieved a weekly mileage of 5,270 miles which equated to 115 hours of running.

During September 1963, after DP2 had clocked up some 220,000 miles of intense running, it was decided to remove the locomotive from service for extended maintenance, which was carried out at the Robert Stephenson Works in Darlington – during the course of which new bogies were installed of a modified design. After its return to service DP2 was again allocated to Finsbury Park, being deployed on a wide variety of ECML duties including Edinburgh, Newcastle and Leeds diagrams.

By the summer of 1965, DP2 became due for its first classified overhaul – this being carried out by EE at Vulcan Foundry Works and completed in late July. During the course of the overhaul DP2 was repainted into standard BR Brunswick green – as applied to the 'Deltic' fleet. DP2's return to passenger service was on 3rd August when it headed the 11.20 King's Cross-Sheffield "Sheffield Pullman" service. For the remainder of 1965 DP2 continued operating on the ECML but at the beginning of 1966 the locomotive was called to its builder's works where new state of the art electronic control equipment, including electronic tractive effort and wheel slip/slide units, were fitted.

Release from Vulcan Foundry after modification came on 15th June 1966 when DP2 returned to Finsbury Park for further proving runs with new equipment. However, prior to operating again on the ER DP2 was used on the LMR between Crewe and Carlisle over the arduous Shap incline where the new electronic control equipment was tested to its full potential. From the late summer of 1966 DP2 was again used on a variety of King's Cross main line services including the Anglo-Scottish car service. It was whilst working this train on 4th August that a derailment occurred outside Edinburgh Waverley which necessitated DP2's removal to Vulcan Foundry until the end of the month.

Between September 1966 and the summer of 1967, DP2 was used on a variety of Eastern Region diagrams including King's Cross-Cambridge, Leeds, Sheffield, York and Anglo-Scottish diagrams, the majority of which were under the watchful eye of EE and BR engineers observing the performance of the electrical equipment.

The premature end for DP2 came on 31st July 1967 whilst heading the 12 noon King's Cross-Edinburgh express. As the Scottish bound train headed north, to the south of Thirsk, the 02.40 Cliffe-Uddingston cement train derailed in its path. Although the driver of DP2 managed to reduce his train's speed to around 50 mph the impact into the derailed wagons was very severe, derailing DP2 and the leading seven coaches of the train. Regrettably seven passengers on the train were killed and 45 seriously injured. DP2's damage was extensive, with the nose end at No. 1 end almost totally destroyed and serious side swipe damage. After recovery from the scene DP2 was taken to York Depot where an inspection was carried out. As the locomotive was privately owned the onus of repair fell to its owner. However, as the cause of the derailment was placed with BR, financial assistance would have been forthcoming. On 8th September the locomotive made its final journey on BR tracks when it returned to Vulcan Foundry and the decision taken to scrap the locomotive. Most of the internal equipment was salvaged for re-use, including the power unit and generator. The main body section was broken up by English Electric staff at Vulcan Foundry in 1968. It is wondered what would have happened to DP2 if it had not been involved in the Thirsk collision – who knows, it may have still been in service today. At the time of its withdrawal DP2 had clocked up 627,000 miles in service.

DP2 awaits departure from King's Cross on 14th September 1965 with empty stock for Ferme Park carriage sidings.
Author's collection

During the early 1960s the 'standard' Type 4 locomotive was rapidly becoming the Brush Type 4, later Class 47. To other construction companies this was, of course, bad news with little chance of breaking into the main line passenger locomotive market, even though companies such as English Electric had built, and were operating the highly successful prototype DP2 and other companies were quite able to produce satisfactory main line power. By 1965 when the Brush build was in full swing, the need for 'high-power' diesel traction became very apparent on the northern sections of the West Coast Main Line between Crewe, Carlisle and Glasgow, which were not covered in the 1960's electrification scheme. Although high-speed schedules would be possible south of Crewe, only very much slower schedules were permissible over the tortuous northern section, using existing motive power.

By far the most suitable answer was to re-equip a batch of existing Brush Type 4 (Class 47) locomotives for high-speed operation, including a multiple operating facility. However at the same time as this consideration was made, a series of major failures befell the Brush fleet and other Sulzer powered locomotives, involving fatigue cracks to power units. This problem unfortunately led to the derating of the Sulzer engines to 2,580hp.

With the above in mind the BRB had a major problem on their hands in terms of motive power, with senior railway managers favouring the Sulzer prime mover, despite its problems, while the London Midland Region mechanical engineers were keen to press for a production batch of DP2 style Type 4s, utilising EE traction technology. After considerable deliberation on future traction policy, tenders were invited in June 1965 for a production run of either 50 or 110 locomotives. Tenders were sought for either a Brush/Sulzer, a Brush/EE partnership, or a totally English Electric product.

A total EE locomotive was of course the most lucrative to English Electric Co. Ltd, who were very keen to break the Brush/Sulzer monopoly. With this in mind EE produced plans for a leasing arrangement with the BRB, whereby the locomotives could be assembled under a contract from the Railways Board, owned by a separate EE company known as 'English Electric Leasings Ltd', and leased to BR. This arrangement would give financial benefit to both parties with the BRB not having to spend vast capital whilst EE could offset a portion of its costs against tax. As well as the leasing arrangement EE were keen to provide a maintenance contract – similar to that in force on the Class 55 'Deltic' locomotives, which would (on paper) provide an 85% availability figure.

Tenders for the fleet were studied during June/July 1965 when many constructional and leasing queries were raised. By November 1965 a decision on the project was reached and a letter of intent raised between the BRB and EE to build and lease a total of 50, DP2 type locomotives to BR, a deal which in 1968 terms was worth around £2.5 million. At this juncture delivery was planned to commence at the beginning of 1967, a date later amended.

At the time of the agreement BR had recently completed the formation of the Railway Technical Centre (RTC) at Derby, which concentrated for the first time the main core

of railway engineers and research functions under one roof. This new establishment was therefore given the brief to refine EE's basic design, for which an advisory committee was formed. Such was the previous success of DP2, there was little need for alterations at all, but alas the committee stipulated the inclusion of new, unproven electronics to govern traction and adhesion characteristics, and in many areas eliminate the need for electro-mechanical devices. Other items covered by the Derby Committee included the provision of rheostatic (dynamic) braking, the fitting of electronic controls to the field weakening system, installing slow speed control (SSC) equipment for merry-go-round operation, the fitting of an electronic management system for the radiator cooling fans, the removal of the steam heat facility, the use of electronic switching equipment for self-extinguishing of internal lights, and the provision of a vigilance type driver's safety device. Whilst not directed for immediate fitting, provisions were required for the accommodation of buckeye couplers, weight transfer equipment and multiple control facilities including push-pull.

After EE became aware of these stipulations imposed by BR a protracted wrangle took place, as it was viewed by EE that BR doubted the company's traction credibility. Concern was also raised by EE regarding a projected guaranteed availability figure of 85% – this was considered possible to attain with production type DP2 locomotives – but with the new BR additions doubts prevailed.

After inter-business problems as to the final detail fittings, the external design of the production locomotives, allocated BR Nos D400-D449, was under the overall direction of Walter Jowett, being finalised in late 1966. Construction of the first locomotive commenced at the English Electric Co. Ltd, Vulcan Foundry Works at Newton-le-Willows in January 1967. By the end of the month frames had been laid for five locomotives and body assembly was quickly started. The first two EE 16CSVT prime movers became available in April and installed into the carcases of Nos D400 and D401 in May. By mid-August construction of the first locomotive was all but cosmetically complete, and on 4th September, No. D400 resplendent in new BR Rail-blue livery, with full yellow warning ends, was passed for main line running, operating a trial run from Vulcan Works to Chester and back. Before the end of 1967 three locomotives had been handed over to BR with the remainder being completed in 1968. The final locomotive of the build, No. D449, being handed over on 30th November 1968.

Construction

The underframe assembly was formed of four longitudinal members, tied by cross-stretchers. Across the frame ends the headstocks carried buffing and drawgear equipment. The body sides were formed of a frame welded to the solebar which in conjunction with bracing bars assisted in underframe rigidity. The outside of the body frames were plated with medium gauge steel plate. The roof section, designed to be removable for easy equipment maintenance, had opening hatches and was formed in steel plate.

At an early stage in the design EE produced a drawing of the projected locomotives front end, incorporating a

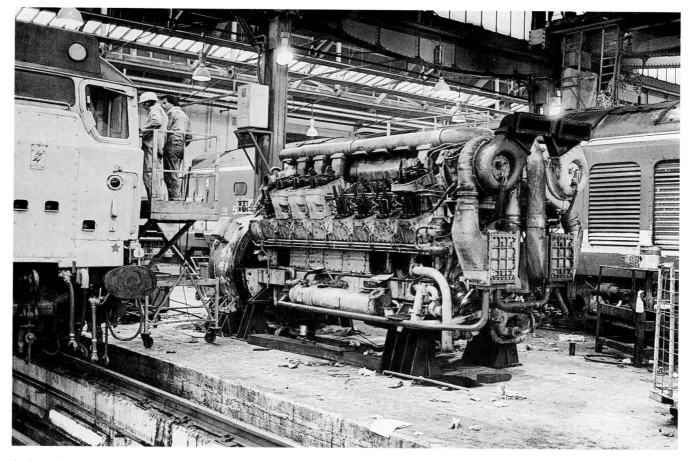

A view of a production EE 16CSVT power unit as installed in the Class 50 fleet. This example, posed on workshop stands at Old Oak Common, is receiving classified attention. Note that some of the cylinder heads are removed. *CJM*

Prior to painting and during its test period at Vulcan Foundry, the eventual No. D400, stands in workshops primer in the Vulcan Foundry yard. The first locomotive of the build has always been identifiable from others by the omission of grab rails above the tail marker lights. *GEC Traction*

curved cab with twin wrap-round screens, and a 4-character route indicator and jumpers positioned below. Regrettably, prior to the locomotive's external design being finalised, a mock-up of a new 'standard' main line cab was produced at the RTC Derby, this conforming with the latest safety requirements stipulated by the MoT Chief Inspecting Officer of Railways. Whilst EE and their designers criticised the new 'standard' cab this had to be incorporated into the D400 series, this requirement leading to the slab-fronted layout we see today, and the position of the route box on the roof line looking like an added extra. The main front panel below the cab window line is basically flat, and incorporating the provision for multiple control jumpers. This equipment, consists of a 36-pin jumper cable and receptacle. When built the first two locomotives were fitted with jumper equipment for trial purposes, whilst the remaining 48 locomotives had all wiring installed but blanking plates fitted over the jumper positions. As the multiple control equipment was unique to this class an orange square restriction code was imposed. As time proved, BR required multiple operation within this fleet during the early 1970s and eventually all 50 locomotives received the equipment. To complete the front end detail, the buffer beam equipment, apart from buffers and coupling, consisted of one vacuum pipe, one air brake pipe, two main reservoir pipes, two engine air control pipes, one ETS jumper socket, and slightly above the buffer beam, one ETS jumper cable.

Moving along the side of the locomotive from the No. 1 end, two air-operated shutter louvres and one fixed air louvre panel are located, these providing entry for cooling air to the radiator system. Prior to refurbishment, sandbox filler ports (never used) were positioned on the cab side and to the rear of the louvre panels (and at similar positions at the opposite end). Along the 'A' side of the locomotive (with No. 1 end on the left) one small oval louvre was located and two oval glazed windows, as well as a cant rail height horizontal ventilator towards the No. 2 end. At the No. 2 end, directly behind the cab area, a ventilator louvre was originally positioned to permit air to ventilate the dynamic brake resistors, this consisting of two panels, the lower third of which was hinged to give access to a blower motor. A recessed roof with air-operated shutters was located above. Following refurbishment the recessed roof has been plated over to provide a conventional profile, whilst the side louvres remained. On the locomotive's 'B' side three windows and one small air louvre were originally provided, but following refurbishment the window

Following the agreement between EE and BR for the fleet of 50 Type 4 locomotives to be built, owned and leased by EE to BR, the EE company placed a construction contract with their Vulcan Foundry Works. The skeleton frame of No. D407 is seen under assembly, while in the background is the near-complete body of No. D406. *GEC Traction*

Completed EE Type 4 No. D437 stands inside the main erecting shop at Vulcan Foundry receiving finishing touches prior to operating a test run and delivery to BR. This aerial view clearly shows the original roof layout, with the cooler group nearest the camera. The open roof hatches show how top engine maintenance could be carried out easily.

GEC Traction

nearest No. 1 end was altered to a louvred panel.

The between-bogie layout consisted of a 1,000 gallon fuel tank, battery box and air compressor.

Bogies

The time-honoured EE cast steel bogie with a 13ft 6in wheelbase was used for the D400s. This was almost identical to the style fitted to the Class 37 and 55 fleets already in traffic. The design was of the equalized beam type, incorporating swing bolsters, the main body-weight being carried on four side bearers on each bolster and transmitted via four spring nests and two spring planks held by links to the bogie frame. One major difference on the D400 bogies was the provision for fitting weight transfer equipment, but this was never installed, except to No. D417 for experimental purposes. Traction motors used were of the EE538/5A type, again similar to those used on the previous Type 3s. Roller bearing suspension provided by SKF/Timkin was fitted and the traction motors themselves were wired in a series/parallel system with three stages of field weakening.

Power Unit and Generator Group

The power unit adopted for the D400 build was of the same type as used in the DP2 prototype – an EE 16CSVT unit which in its latest form was a turbo-charged, air-cooled unit, developing 2,700hp at 850rpm, the normal engine idling speed being 450rpm. The design of this engine differed little from the type used in the 1940's EE prototypes and is a 'V' form unit with 8 cylinders in each bank. Four Napier 'HP' series turbo-chargers are located on the top corners. When ordered for the D400s a total of 52 engines were constructed, allocated EE numbers IH6845-49, and IH6927-73.

Coupled to the flange of the power unit is an EE built EE840/1B type main generator, a 12-pole machine rated at 1,746kW at 850rpm. Coupled to the free end of this generator is the electric train supply generator of Type EE915-1B, this being an 8-pole self-ventilated machine rated at 320kW. In addition to train supply this unit provides power for the radiator fan motor. As the train supply generator was unable to operate at idling speed, whenever train supply is selected the engine speed is automatically increased. Overhung from the rear of the ETS generator is the auxiliary generator of type EE911-5C, this being an 8-pole machine with a rating of 66kW and provides power to all auxiliary electric circuits.

Towards the end of the construction of the Class 50s, an order was placed with English Electric to supply ten 2,700hp units for the 5ft 6in gauge Portuguese Railways. As the company was geared up for this production the Portuguese examples resembled the Class 50s in many ways, including the power unit and cooler group type. The upper view shows the first of the build in the Vulcan Foundry erecting shop, No. 1801, while the lower view shows the locomotive being lowered onto the deck of the SS *Ida-Jacobi* at Manchester Docks in December 1968, for its shipment to Lisbon.

Author's collection

Although officially owned by a company known as English Electric Leasings Ltd, the EE Type 4, later Class 50 fleet were outshopped in the new BR standard 'Rail blue' livery from new, with D prefix numbers below all four cab side windows, together with double arrow logos. The pioneer member of the class, No. D400 is seen under the water test apparatus at Vulcan Foundry, where high pressure water jets simulated rain to establish if any body water leaks existed. *GEC Traction*

To indicate ownership by English Electric Leasings Ltd a cast plate was carried on both sides of the locomotives in a mid-body position. *Brian Morrison*

Technical Description

DP2

Number	DP2
Built by	EE Vulcan Foundry
Introduced	1962
Wheel Arrangement	Co-Co
Weight	105 tonnes
Height	12ft 10in
Width	8ft 9½in
Length	69ft 6in
Min. Curve negotiable	4 chains
Maximum Speed	90mph
Wheelbase	58ft 6in
Bogie Wheelbase	13ft 6in
Bogie Pivot Centres	45ft
Wheel Diameter	3ft 7in
Brake Type	Vacuum
Sanding Equipment	Pneumatic
Route Availability	6
Heating Type	Steam – Clayton RO 2000 (as built), later type RO 2500
Multiple Coupling Restriction	Not MU fitted
Brake Force	52 tonnes
Engine Type	EE 16CSVT
Engine Horsepower	2,700hp
Power at Rail	2,070hp
Tractive Effort	55,000lb
Cylinder Bore	10in
Cylinder Stroke	12in
Main Generator Type	EE 840-1B
Aux. Generator Type	EE 911-5C
Number of Traction Motors	6
Traction Motor Type	EE 538A
Gear Ratio	53:18
Fuel Tank Capacity	900gal
Cooling Water Capacity	280gal
Lub Oil Capacity	130gal
Boiler Water Capacity	620gal

Class 50

Class		50
Former Class Code		27/3
Number Range		
TOPS	(50/0)	50001-50050
	(50/1)	50149
Former Number Range		D400-D449
Built by		EE Vulcan Foundry
Introduced	(50/0)	1967-68
	(50/1)	1987
Wheel Arrangement		Co-Co
Weight (operational)		117 tonnes
Height		12ft 10¾in
Width		9ft 1¼in
Length		68ft 6in
Min. Curve negotiable		4 chains
Maximum Speed	(50/0)	100mph*
	(50/1)	80mph
Wheelbase		56ft 2in
Bogie Wheelbase		13ft 6in
Bogie Pivot Centres		42ft 8in
Wheel Diameter		3ft 7in
Brake Type		Dual
Sanding Equipment		Not fitted
Heating Type		Electric – Index 61
Route Availability		6
Multiple Coupling Restriction		Orange Square
Brake Force		59 tonnes
Engine Type		EE16CSVT
Engine Horsepower		2,700hp
Power at Rail		2,070hp
Tractive Effort		48,500lb
Cylinder Bore		10in
Cylinder Stroke		12in
Main Generator Type		EE840-4B
Aux. Generator Type		EE911-5C
ETS Generator Type		EE915-1B
Number of Traction Motors		6
Traction Motor Type		EE538-5A
Gear Ratio	(50/0)	53:18
	(50/1)	59:16
Fuel Tank Capacity		1,055gal
Cooling Water Capacity		280gal
Lub Oil Capacity		130gal

Details for 50/1 apply to locomotive No. 50149 between 8/87 and 2/89 only.

*60 mph speed restrictions have been imposed on Departmental-owned locomotives from 1989.

Cab Layout

The production cab layout of the EE Type 4 conformed to the 1966 standard locomotive cab design, a layout agreed with BR, trade unions, medical advisers and major production companies, to offer the driver the best possible working environment. The upper illustration shows the original 'as built' layout, while the lower plate shows a refurbished locomotive complete with cab to shore radio/telephone. Note how the positions of a number of items has been changed.

1. Locomotive brake valve, 2. Train brake valve (proportional on loco), 3. AWS re-set button, 4. AWS sunflower indicator, 5. Brake pipe gauge, 6. Bogie brake cylinder pressure gauge, 7. Vacuum gauge, 8. Speedometer, 9. Tractive effort pre-select dial, 10. Main generator ampmeter, 11. Slow speed control speedometer, 12. Slow speed control setting switch, 13. Main reservoir pressure gauge, 14. Wheelslip indicator light, 15. Overload re-set button, 16. Engine start button, 17. Engine stop button, 18. General fault alarm, 19. Engine stopped indicator, 20. Fire alarm test button, 21. Train heat 'on' indicator, 22. Train heat indicator dimmer switch, 23. Train heat 'on' button, 24. Driver's side windscreen wiper valve, 25. Driver's side windscreen washer button, 26. Indicator light switch, 27. Wheelslip brake button, 28. Horn valve, 29. Master switch, 30. Power controller, 31. Cab ventilation control, 32. Handle for operating train reporting numbers, 33. Vigilance device alarm, 34. Headlight switch, 35. Cab-shore radio telephone.

Both CJM

Fleet List

BR 1957 No.	TOPS No.	Re No. Date	Name	Name Date	Depot	Sector	Builder's Nos English Electric/ Vulcan Foundry	Date Introduced
D400	50050	2/74	*Fearless*	23/8/78	LA	NSSA	3770/D1141	October 1967
D401	50001	2/74	*Dreadnought*	10/4/78	LA	NSSA	3772/D1143	December 1967
D402	50002	4/74	*Superb*	21/3/78	LA	NSSA	3771/D1142	December 1967
D403	50003	2/74	*Temeraire*	9/5/78	LA	NSSA	3773/D1144	January 1968
D404	50004	2/74	*St Vincent*	9/5/78	LA	–	3774/D1145	December 1967
D405	50005	8/74	*Collingwood*	5/4/78	LA	NSSA	3775/D1146	January 1968
D406	50006	3/74	*Neptune*	25/9/79	–	–	3776/D1147	April 1968
D407	50007	4/74	*Sir Edward Elgar*	25/2/84	LA	NSSA	3777/D1148	March 1968
D408	50008	2/74	*Thunderer*	01/9/78	LA	DCWA	3778/D1149	March 1968
D409	50009	12/73	*Conqueror*	8/5/78	LA	DCWA	3779/D1150	March 1968
D410	50010	3/74	*Monarch*	16/3/78	–	–	3780/D1151	March 1968
D411	50011	2/74	*Centurion*	17/8/79	–	–	3781/D1152	April 1968
D412	50012	2/74	*Benbow*	3/4/78	–	–	3782/D1153	April 1968
D413	50013	5/74	*Agincourt*	19/4/78	–	–	3783/D1154	April 1968
D414	50014	4/74	*Warspite*	30/5/78	–	–	3784/D1155	May 1968
D415	50015	2/74	*Valiant*	21/4/78	LA	DCWA	3785/D1156	April 1968
D416	50016	12/73	*Barham*	3/4/78	LA	NSSA	3786/D1157	May 1968
D417	50017	2/74	*Royal Oak*	24/4/78	LA	NSSA	3787/D1158	April 1968
D418	50018	2/74	*Resolution*	18/4/78	LA	NSSA	3788/D1159	April 1968
D419	50019	12/73	*Ramillies*	18/4/78	–	–	3789/D1160	May 1968
D420	50020	2/74	*Revenge*	7/7/78	–	–	3790/D1161	May 1968
D421	50021	11/73	*Rodney*	31/7/78	–	–	3791/D1162	May 1968
D422	50022	3/74	*Anson*	2/4/78	–	–	3792/D1163	May 1968
D423	50023	12/73	*Howe*	17/5/78	–	–	3793/D1164	June 1968
D424	50024	2/74	*Vanguard*	14/4/78	LA	NSSA	3794/D1165	June 1968
D425	50025	2/74	*Invincible*	6/6/78	–	–	3795/D1166	July 1968
D426	50026	2/74	*Indomitable*	29/3/78	LA	NSSA	3796/D1167	July 1968
D427	50027	1/74	*Lion*	17/4/78	LA	NSSA	3797/D1168	June 1968
D428	50028	2/74	*Tiger*	16/5/78	LA	NSSA	3798/D1169	July 1968
D429	50029	3/74	*Renown*	26/11/78	LA	NSSA	3799/D1170	July 1968
D430	50030	3/74	*Repulse*	10/4/78	LA	NSSA	3800/D1171	July 1968
D431	50031	2/74	*Hood*	28/6/78	LA	DCWA	3801/D1172	July 1968
D432	50032	2/74	*Courageous*	7/7/78	–	–	3802/D1173	July 1968
D433	50033	4/74	*Glorious*	26/6/78	LA	NSSA	3803/D1174	August 1968
D434	50034	3/74	*Furious*	6/4/78	–	–	3804/D1175	August 1968
D435	50035	3/74	*Ark Royal*	10/1/78	–	–	3805/D1176	August 1968
D436	50036	10/73	*Victorious*	16/5/78	LA	DCWA	3806/D1177	September 1968
D437	50037	2/74	*Illustrious*	8/6/78	LA	NSSA	3807/D1178	September 1968
D438	50038	2/74	*Formidable*	5/5/78	–	–	3808/D1179	October 1968
D439	50039	2/74	*Implacable*	26/6/78	–	–	3809/D1180	October 1968
D440	50040	2/74	*Centurion*	5/7/87	–	–	3810/D1181	October 1968
D441	50041	3/74	*Bulwark*	8/5/78	–	–	3811/D1182	October 1968
D442	50042	12/73	*Triumph*	4/10/78	LA	DCWA	3812/D1183	October 1968
D443	50043	2/74	*Eagle*	28/6/78	LA	NSSA	3813/D1184	October 1968
D444	50044	2/74	*Exeter*	26/4/78	LA	NSSA	3814/D1185	November 1968
D445	50045	3/74	*Achilles*	12/4/78	LA	NSSA	3815/D1186	November 1968
D446	50046	2/74	*Ajax*	11/10/78	LA	NSSA	3816/D1187	December 1968
D447	50047	2/74	*Swiftsure*	26/5/78	–	–	3817/D1188	December 1968
D448	50048	3/74	*Dauntless*	16/3/78	LA	NSSA	3818/D1189	December 1968
D449	50049	2/74	*Defiance*	02/5/78	LA	NSSA	3819/D1190	December 1968

With a mixed rake of NSE and InterCity stock behind 'more yellow' No. 50008 *Thunderer*, passes over the picturesque Cockwood Harbour between Dawlish Warren and Starcross on 20th July 1988 with the 11.59 Portsmouth Harbour-Plymouth service.

CJM

BR 1957 No.	Depot of Original Allocation	Date Withdrawn	Depot of Final Allocation	Disposal Code	Disposal Detail	Date Cut up	Notes
D400	LMWL	–	–	–	–	–	–
D401	LMWL	–	–	–	–	–	–
D402	LMWL	–	–	–	–	–	–
D403	LMWL	–	–	–	–	–	–
D404	LMWL	22/6/90	LA	A	BR Laira	–	–
D405	LMWL	–	–	–	–	–	–
D406	LMWL	1/7/87	LA	C	V. Berry, Leicester	3/88	–
D407	LMWL	–	–	–	–	–	Named *Hercules* 6/4/78 – 5/2/84
D408	LMWL	–	–	–	–	–	–
D409	LMWL	–	–	–	–	–	–
D410	LMWL	27/9/88	LA	A	BR Laira	–	–
D411	LMWL	24/2/87	LA	A	BREL Ltd Crewe	–	–
D412	LMWL	16/1/89	LA	A	V Berry, Leicester	5/89	–
D413	LMWL	31/3/88	LA	C	BR Old Oak Common	6/89	By V. Berry
D414	LMWL	14/12/87	LA	C	V. Berry, Leicester	5/89	–
D415	LMWL	–	–	–	–	–	–
D416	LMWL	3/8/90	LA	A	BR Laira	–	–
D417	LMWL	–	–	–	–	–	–
D418	LMWL	–	–	–	–	–	–
D419	LMWL	14/9/90	LA	A	BR Laira	–	–
D420	LMWL	27/7/90	LA	A	BR Laira	–	–
D421	LMWL	17/4/90	LA	A	BR Laira	–	–
D422	LMWL	20/9/88	OC	C	V. Berry, Leicester	5/89	–
D423	LMWL	10/90	LA	A	BR Laira	–	–
D424	LMWL	–	–	–	–	–	–
D425	LMWL	14/8/89	OC	C	BR Old Oak Common	10/89	By V. Berry
D426	D05	–	–	–	–	–	–
D427	D05	–	–	–	–	–	–
D428	D05	–	–	–	–	–	–
D429	D05	–	–	–	–	–	–
D430	D05	–	–	–	–	–	–
D431	D05	–	–	–	–	–	–
D432	D05	10/90	LA	A	BR Old Oak Common	–	–
D433	D05	–	–	–	–	–	–
D434	D05	29/6/90	OC	A	BR Old Oak Common	–	–
D435	D05	3/8/90	LA	A	BR Old Oak Common	–	–
D436	D05	–	–	–	–	–	–
D437	D05	–	–	–	–	–	–
D438	D05	27/9/88	OC	C	BR Old Oak Common	8/89	By V. Berry
D439	D05	4/6/89	OC	A	BR Old Oak Common	–	–
D440	D05	3/8/90	LA	A	BR Laira	–	Named *Leviathan* 15/9/78 –6/7/87
D441	D05	17/4/90	LA	A	BR Old Oak Common	–	–
D442	D05	–	–	–	–	–	–
D443	D05	–	–	–	–	–	–
D444	D05	–	–	–	–	–	–
D445	D05	–	–	–	–	–	–
D446	D05	–	–	–	–	–	–
D447	D05	13/4/88	LA	C	V. Berry, Leicester	7/89	–
D448	D05	–	–	–	–	–	–
D449	D05	–	–	–	–	–	Numbered 50149 8/87–02/89

Codes:
LA – Laira
OC – Old Oak Common
A – Awaiting disosal
C – Cut up
LMWL – London Midland Western Lines
D05 – LM Crewe division
NSSA – NSE Waterloo - Exeter Line
DCWA – WR Departmental (LA)

During the early 1970s the use of double-headed Class 50s on Anglo-Scottish services north of Crewe became the norm, until displaced by electrification. On 17th July 1971 Nos 419 and 429 descend Shap at Greenholme with a southbound express. To the rear of the train a start on electrification work can be seen.
G. T. Heavyside

In Detail

Class 50 front end layout. A few end alterations have occurred during the careers of these locomotives, namely the removal of the 4-character route indicator equipment, its replacement with two marker lights, and the provision of a sealed beam high-intensity headlight centrally on the nose end.

1. Air horns behind grille, 2. Marker lights, 3. Red tail light, 4. Headlight, 5. Multiple control jumper, 6. Multiple control jumper receptacle, 7. ETS socket, 8. ETS jumper cable, 9. Air brake pipe, 10. Main reservoir pipe, 11. Engine control air pipe, 12. Vacuum pipe.

CJM

Bogie and bodyside detail at No. 2 end of refurbished Class 50, showing the alterations made to the roof during refurbishment work.

CJM

Roof detail of English Electric 'prototype' No. DP2.

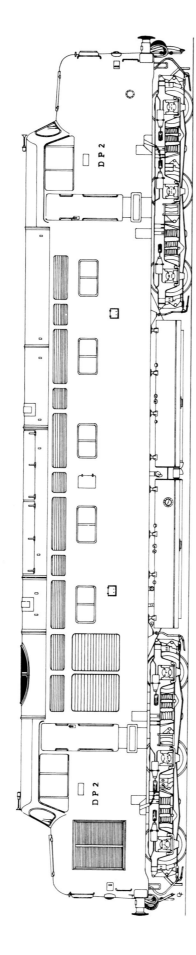

Side elevation of English Electric second generation 'prototype' No. DP2, with No. 1 end on the left.

Scale: $3\frac{1}{2}$mm = 1ft

(All drawings by Graham B. Fenn)

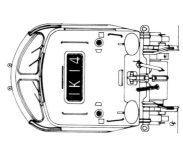

Front end elevation of No. DP2, clearly showing the near identical appearances to the production 'Deltic' type.

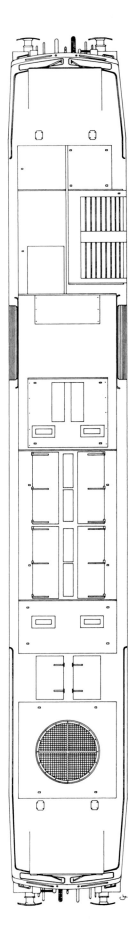

Roof detail, unrefurbished

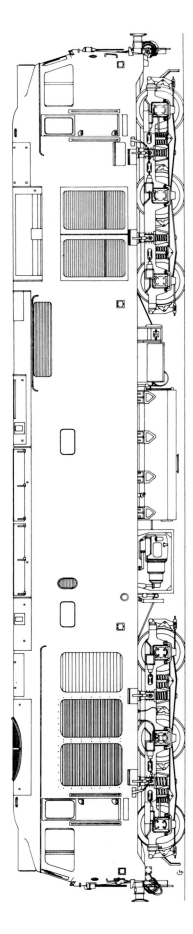

Side elevation, unrefurbished.

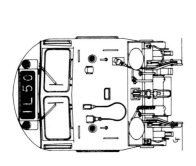

Front end detail, showing refurbished layout.

Front end detail, showing unrefurbished layout.

Roof detail, refurbished.

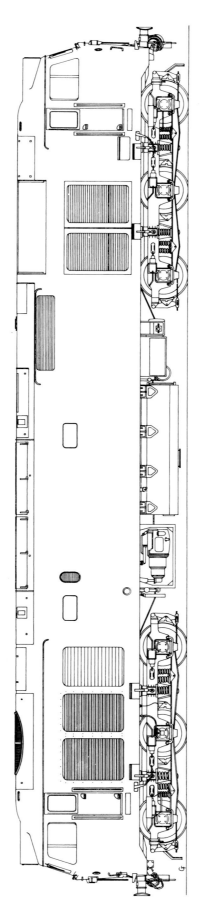

Side elevation, refurbished. No. 1 end to the left.

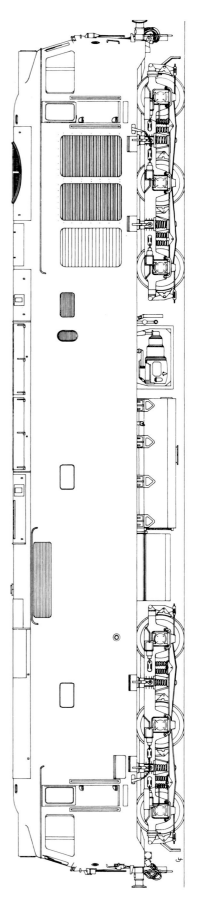

Side elevation, refurbished, No. 1 end to the right.

Performance — The Last Search For Identity

by Michael Oakley

Not everybody believes that machines can have minds of their own, but in railway locomotion, at any rate, there is a certain suspicion of it. Subtle differences in the designed performance of rival machines can become elaborated, with familiarity, into pronounced strengths and weaknesses out on the road, with the result that reputations are acquired of suitability for different tasks. Although a quite unjustified multitude of different designs appeared on BR in the modernisation period, the intention at least of achieving horses for courses can be distinguished, fighting always against the concept of adaptability. The horses won in the end, but the legacy of the argument can still be enjoyed as it keeps a good part of BR going.

Nowhere does one have to look more carefully to the subtleties of performance than in the Type 4 power category. Once the engineers got away from the fairly primitive 2,000 bhp machine (later Class 40) which no more than equalled steam performance, and up to a power/weight ratio half as good again, a whole new general standard was set. The six-axle general-purpose locomotive of around 2,700 bhp rapidly became the accepted big engine design, and there has been more than a tendency to treat similar locomotives as having similar capabilities. The truth is both more subtle and more curious. If one looks at the actual performance characteristics designed in, they seem to have been given a lot of thought to start with, and then less as they went on.

A great deal of argument, mainly financial, centred around the Western Region diesel-hydraulics of all sizes. More expensive to maintain and create, they were claimed by their promoters to offer superior performance which made it worthwhile. In theory they certainly did, and the characteristic performance curve of a hydraulic – exceptionally strong off the mark, weak in the range of the middle converter, strong again around the designed maximum, then a sudden dramatic fall-off – came to be appreciated by far more people than mechanical engineers. It was said of the West of England main line in particular that the hydraulics were ideal for it – which they certainly were when cruising at 90 mph out of Paddington or restarting 500 tons up the 1 in 47 out of Totnes. Pity about the 138 miles from Reading to Exeter where they were shown at their weakest; one simply cannot have it all ways.

The other extreme, by comparison, was the Brush Class 47, eventually adopted as "standard", though in its detail variations it was nothing of the sort. Trying to squeeze more out of a system that had reached its limit, this fell between two stools where extremes of work were required. Weak at low speed, with a continuous rating as high as 27 mph, the 47 was found wanting on heavy freight work and damage through overloading at low speed became intolerable. Weak at high speed, with electrical unloading starting at 82 mph and having a more marked effect than on the earlier 'Peaks' (Classes 45 and 46), a 47 will run freely up to 3-figure speeds on long downgrades, but fall off rapidly at the first upturn. Not helped by derating to 2,580 bhp from 2,750, the 47s might well have proved happier suited to the West of England trains, leaving the Swanseas to the hydraulics, the reverse of what actually happened.

This die had largely been cast when English Electric

returned to the fray with the DP2 experiment, which was very much a solution in search of a problem. Once they had nosed ahead again, or so they claimed anyway, in design superiority, it was probably a business necessity to establish a presence on the road, in spite of no particular gap in the market existing. By default, therefore, DP2 became the last throw in the "mixed-traffic" argument. It was probably just because it was available, rather than for any specific traffic objective, that this locomotive and the subsequent production series acquired 100 mph maximum speed, controlled tractive effort, and a performance curve rather more like a 52 than a 47. It was probably equally a coincidence that the 50s in time became the direct replacements for the 52s, the demise of the latter being not for shape but for lack of performance.

In any case, BR put the DP2 locomotive through a brief assortment of tests, but then used it solely for express work on the East Coast Main Line. This it seems to have accomplished admirably, performance coming out much as designed, with an overall higher-geared effect than most of its contemporaries. The tragedy of its demise left unanswered the question of what its freight capabilities, under the pressure of prolonged intensive usage, might have been.

For what it may be worth, anyway, BR chose the design for a production series when more power was needed for Crewe to Glasgow. The general run of work was full-size expresses but plenty of room to work them up to high speed. The specific obstacles of Shap and Beattock would require collar work down to about 40 mph (30 mph on the heaviest night trains, although they were timed easily) at the other extreme. The job matched the locomotive, slightly better than the 47s it replaced, and at first the performances out on the road were improved in proportion. Table 1 is a typical run of the Crewe period, with a full-size express but also a full-tilt run at the banks. Although this run was making up time on an easy Sunday schedule, the weekday timings were demanding, and flat-out running all the way was usually to be expected. The way speed held up on the upper part of Beattock bank was particularly impressive, noticeably better than up Shap. Discreet enquiries on arrival did not establish whether the driver had switched off the electric train heating, contrary to instructions, but crews had been changed at Carlisle, so it was a distinct possibility! It certainly would not have been the only time. Fortunately the BR ETH indexing system introduced thereafter makes it possible to estimate at least the maximum effect of heating and air-conditioning, if not the actual one, and in this case a maximum effect of 350 hp is close to the 250 hp difference between the equivalent drawbar horsepower for Shap and Beattock at similar speeds. 2,125 edhp at 47 mph corresponds to about 2,270 rail hp, against a figure of 2,195 from the tractive effort curve. That is a little outside the normal margin for error, and may be taken as a slightly over-par performance.

Unfortunately the production series locomotives failed to stand up to intensive usage as the prototype had done. In their defence it is claimed that usage was over-intensive, leaving insufficient time for proper maintenance when emergencies had to be covered anyhow. Then again, the shortages tended to be caused in the first place by other

problems in the same locomotives. The production series were a box of tricks in many ways that the prototype was not, and first experiences with new-fangled electronic control systems included some unhappy ones. The tractive effort pre-set was seldom needed or used, since the locomotives were sure-footed anyway and quickly into their stride on passenger work. Another problem was traction motor flashovers, probably no worse than in any other diesel-electric, but the series-parallel wiring meant two motors had to be isolated together, with power loss in proportion. Worst of all were the field divert failures, when the system, which changed the generator field current so as to widen its performance range, would go on strike. This had the same effect as mechanical gearing, when the locomotive would work perfectly in whatever part of the performance range it had reached, but tail away to nothing when it reached the next critical speed.

Table 2 is an example of the dismal level to which things sank at times, No. D426 having the worst reputation overall, but No. D403 being responsible for the writer's worst individual performance. Once again the shape of the performance is significant, as well as the overall level. Even with this above-average load, a speed of 90 mph ought to have been possible approaching Crewe, and certainly the output leaving Warrington, though poor, was much too high for a pair of motors to be isolated. Once past about 58 mph, however, this being the speed at which the third and final stage of field-weakening occurs, performance fell away to little more than half what it should have been. That in turn is still better than if the weak-field had not operated, so the resulting performance is a puzzle which could have had various causes.

With such inconsistency rampant, it is not surprising that the next development was another disappointment. In the search for higher speeds pending electrification, it was decided to double-head the principal daytime expresses. Locomotives should have been available, as daytime traffic on the West Coast Main Line is always lighter than at night when most heavy freight is moved, and at first the arrangement worked well. Then, increasingly, locomotives became in short supply, and single-heading with loss of time resulted. Consistently, the analysis of performances revealed they were nowhere near twice as good with two locomotives instead of one. Individual performances would occasionally sparkle, but so rarely that no instances are known of two locomotives together putting out a par 4000 hp at the drawbar. Minimum speeds in the 70s up Shap and Beattock were common, but so were those in the 60s, which barely justified the extravagance. Reaching 100 mph on the level when double-headed was easy enough, even with poor locomotives double-headed. Timekeeping was no worse than it might have been, so the situation drifted on erratically for some years.

Perhaps the nadir was the train which arrived very late at Crewe from the North double-headed, and the exasperated driver declared to his relief that he had one pair of motors "out" on the one locomotive and two on the second – the second being inevitably the abominable 426. Only latterly did things improve again, and the best example on record of a truly flat-out acceleration is Table 3. This was a Sunday diversion that had come the sort of route which keeps railway atlas compilers in business (Ais Gill, Clitheroe, Entwistle, Ashton Moss). It was interesting if only for the grotesque experience of coming down through Bromley Cross at 72 mph, which is something that could not happen today. Only on reaching Stockport did it have a chance to run, actually two chances due to a permanent way slowing. This performance is equivalent to reaching 100 mph from a standing start on the level in about five minutes, which was better than anything happening on the normal route at that time. Even so, the horsepower figures were that depressing percentage down on what they might have been. Not surprisingly it became rumoured, although never confirmed, that output settings were being messed with. Still, they survived, and the eventual best-known performance up Beattock, already described in Table 1, was actually recorded on the very last day of the diesel timetable, with electrics already alongside. The 50s left Crewe having hardly worked anything except express passenger trains in all their time there.

On the Western Region, the crisis had been a long time coming. The performance of the hydraulics, which had always varied between the occasionally brilliant and the generally dismal out on the road, had become unacceptably low in terms of mechanical reliability as well. Amid recriminations about further alleged deratings and claims that the British Railways Board had never allowed them to be maintained properly, the decision was taken to scrap the lot. The availability of the Class 50s made surplus at Crewe was obviously a factor, and once again the fact that they were supposedly general-purpose locomotives of the same nominal power as the Class 52 'Westerns' seems to have been given no specific consideration. What was a factor was an increasing perception of the cost of mass crew retraining, so that the new arrivals were started off with the Paddington to Bristol run, leaving South Wales to the 47s. It could be argued that the heavier South Wales

Now BR owned, refurbished and painted in the distinctive 'more yellow' livery, No 50041 *Bulwark* approaches the site of the long closed Kingkerswell station on 25th August 1987 with the 12.03 Portsmouth Harbour-Paignton. Note the train is formed of Network SouthEast stock.

CJM

trains with their longer non-stop runs would have been a slightly better use for them, although in the event erratic individual performance in all classes made more difference than anything else.

Table 4 is typical of the best work at this period. Once into its stride, any Type 4 locomotive could maintain high cruising speed on the gently falling gradients from Swindon to Paddington. The main difference was that a 95 mph limit Class 47 would tail off rapidly as speed got into the 90s (and a 90 mph Class 52 hydraulic even more suddenly at about 95, if a driver tried to push one past the limit). The usual superiority of a 50 was in the evenness of the acceleration up to the full 100 mph; its lack of superiority would be shown in sometimes disappointing climbs of Box and Dauntsey banks at lower speed. Still, with a clear road, startling end-to-end averages could sometimes be achieved. When, several times subsequently, High Speed Trains were in short supply and 50s had to substitute, there was a great deal of sustained 100 mph running in both directions, which looked very good on paper, even if it required no wonderful horsepower output. An eight-coach train of MkII stock, which was the usual load for these substitutions, requires less than 1,000 drawbar horsepower to keep it going at 100 mph on the level, and it is important to look to the accelerations to see where the real work was being done.

A somewhat different job is the West of England main line, which is a test for locomotives at all speeds. Loads were generally heavier, and at the time of the 50s' arrival, the Berks & Hants line and beyond were still mostly in leftover-from-steam condition. Constant changes of gradient make this a difficult route over which to appreciate the performance. Also, not for the first time, it was only after they had been mostly superseded by High Speed Trains that 50s on residual workings were able to show what they could really do on the route. It deserves to be recorded that the enormous upgrading of this route in the 1980s transformed locomotive achievements over it as well. Instead of a cruising average of perhaps 75 mph, the route currently gives scope for three-figure speeds in various places. It is a great pity that schedules between Reading and Taunton in

particular have never exploited this, so that it became dismally commonplace for trains to be trundling at lower speeds than before, after getting well ahead of time.

Table 5 is an example of the remaining summer Saturday workings with a moderate load but also a moderate locomotive. It just managed a full 100 mph on the level at Slough and was unable to hold it up a gradient no steeper than 1 in 1,320. Once onto the downgrades beyond Savernake, however, the high-geared effect remained evident, and a top speed of 106 mph was run up with surprising ease. Using the plunges through the dips around Somerton, previously speed-restricted, produced another 100 mph, and several more might have been possible if the locomotive had not then been eased slightly. The performance on the main climb of the route, to Whiteball Tunnel, steepening to 1 in 80, was well short of previous best, which just shows how much further potential there might be. It is one of the great frustrations of locomotive performance recording that the combination of a clear road, a good 50, and a driver who will run, never just seems to come together.

Another route where the 50s never appeared quite to get it together fully was the Lickey route, on which cross-country services via Birmingham are concentrated. Trains changing to/from electric haulage at Birmingham made a convenient, out-and-home trip for a 50 based at Plymouth, and a greater proportion of stops tended to result in harder running. This was simply because drivers had less scope to build up time in hand, in spite of easier schedules still. The job certainly seemed to be treated as easy by Laira shed, as there were an alarming number of 50s sent to Birmingham with only four motors working, and suspiciously often on the same train. Sitting by the lineside at Blackwell, it was possible to hear the power being adjusted by drivers fighting the ammeter to keep going up the Incline. They always did keep going, one consistency about the 50s being their sure-footedness, but minimum speeds in the region of 10 mph did not exactly benefit their reputation. They also had an inconsistent but fascinating spell working the very heavy Bristol to Glasgow sleeping car train as far as Birmingham – but in this case with a Lickey banker.

One of the best performances on record, just to show that they can do it, is the run in Table 6. This train changed locomotives at Gloucester. No. 50011 always had a good reputation, in spite of – or possibly a factor in – its early demise. The vicious South Devon banks can never really be charged, and here most of all a locomotive needs to keep its feet. Drawbar horsepower figures back over 2,000 where they belong are particularly gratifying on such a road. Not quite so good was the climb to Whiteball, but high

In recent years, one of the main stamping grounds for the Class 50s has been the Waterloo-Salisbury-Exeter line, where performance has generally been good, providing the ability to trim several minutes off the previous Class 33 schedules. On 28th April 1987 No. 50049 *Defiance* hauls the 08.11 Exeter St Davids-Waterloo service past Raynes Park.
CJM

speed was easily attained on the down-grades past Charfield. Subsequent raising of speeds limits has made this a 100 mph route to rival the Berks & Hants as well, while the use of air-conditioned stock gives maximum demand on trains of up to 13 vehicles.

Nevertheless, and with the usual irony, the 50s have fallen from favour just when they might have done their best work of all. Continuing slight mechanical unreliability has told against them, while less erratic performances on the road in the 1980s than in the 1970s have not made much difference. In early 1989 there was a curious debate over how best to work the Salisbury line. Class 50s made surplus by High Speed Train introduction have made this route their own for some time, and their speed off the mark with moderate loads has meant that no other type can match them on the sharp gradients encountered. On the other hand timekeeping has been dismal due in good measure to the stupid way line singling was carried out in the 1960s. If nothing else, the 50s deserve mention for discrediting the one long loop style of line singling, which admitted defeat when Tisbury acquired passing facilities again in the 1980s.

By that time there had been one disruptive locomotive failure too many, and in 1989 Class 47s were tried on a regular basis instead. They were immediately found to be no more reliable – as must be expected of other people's cast-offs – and weaker as usual at low and high speed.

Meanwhile the old order continues, and Table 7 is an example of an average locomotive driven consistently hard. The achievement of "even time" (mile-a-minute average) in about five minutes from rest on the level is something no 47 can match, and the timekeeping edge of a passable 50 is sustainable even when the power output is distinctly down. It was distinctly down leaving Basingstoke on this particular run. When we had reached 67 mph, a signal check intervened causing a sudden shut-off. This is one thing to which a 50 appears vulnerable sometimes, and although the signals cleared, the power stayed at a minimal level. Possibly the driver was anticipating further checks, it was not possible to confirm, but more likely this was a classic example of the old Class 50 weakness, a field diversion failure. When power did come back on, it did so suddenly, and away we went again, with no discernible change of engine note to the recorder in the front coach.

How are we to form an overall judgement of such inconsistent locomotives? Certainly no one or seven individual runs prove anything, and when a final story comes to be written, it will be necessary to look at average achievement over a wide spread. Although only a tiny fraction of performances are ever recorded properly, the way they do rapidly start to average out is comforting, and Table 8 is an attempt to put Class 50 performance in a proper perspective. Whiteball bank is one of the few places where everybody can be relied upon to open out their locomotive. Also there is not too much variation in loadings, so the performances are not too far apart on the speed range for an immediate impression to be gained. The good start, subsequent fall-off, and recent erratic recovery of Class 50 performance on the Western is shown up particularly well here. By comparison the even greater unpredictability of the 47s (contrary to reputation) continues, the brilliance of the 'Peaks' is unsurpassed, and it is shown once and for all just how awful the hydraulics became at their worst. At their best the 50s stand comparison with any of them. They should be remembered as not the only locomotives which ever had problems.

Table 1 Sunday 5th May 1974
13.20 Euston to Glasgow
Locomotive: 50022
Load: 12 vehicles Mk II air-con. stock, 399/430 tons, ETH 54.

m c			m s	speeds
0-00	PRESTON		0.00	–
4-60	Barton		6.25	73
9-38	Garstang		9.53	85
15-20	Bay Horse		13.55	89/91
19-74	Lancaster Old Jn		17.19	sigs 46/28
20-79	Lancaster		19.06	50
27-19	Carnforth		24.15	84/87
30-39	Milepost 9½		26.39	76/86
34-42	Milnthorpe		29.36	83
40-10	Oxenholme		34.06	67/68
43-43	Hey Fell		37.17	62
47-09	Grayrigg		40.54	57/83
53-11	Tebay		45.49	81
56-11	Scout Green		48.18	62
58-48	Shap Summit		51.04	48/81
63-75	Thrimby Grange		55.38	73*
68-01	Clifton		58.41	93/96
72-16	Penrith		61.49	68*/sigs*
79-34	Calthwaite		67.04	90/97
85-14	Wreay		70.51	80*/89
90-08	CARLISLE	=75¼	76.32	–

Table 1 continued:

m c		m s	speeds
2-06	Kingmoor box	3.16	61
6-04	Floriston	6.31	85/86
8-58	Gretna Jn	8.26	83
14-40	Milepost 14½	12.56	74/85
20-10	Ecclefechan	17.09	80/81/77
25-67	Lockerbie	21.11	94
28-58	Nethercleugh	23.00	98
33-40	Milepost 33½	26.04	91/95
39-59	Beattock	30.18	79
45-31	Greskine	35.45	49
49-55	Beattock Summit	41.36	44
52-49	Elvanfoot	43.16	88/92
57-68	Abington	47.49	87/92
63-18	Lamington	51.25	91/88
66-66	Symington	53.50	90/98
70-03	Leggatfoot	55.52	93/100
73-49	Carstairs	58.03	94
78-37	Craigenhill	61.27	85/95
84-06	Law Jn	65.11	67*/96
89-36	Motherwell	69.12	76*/85
93-67	Uddingston	72.32	81*/82
95-56	Newton	74.01	66*/81
99-10	Rutherglen	76.48	75/sigs 0
102-27	GLASGOW CENTRAL = 82½	83.40	–

*speed restrictions
Calculated horsepower output:
1 in 75 rise Tebay to Shap Summit: 1,875 edhp at 60.8 mph.
1 in 200 rise Gretna Jn to MP 14½: 1,785 edhp at 77.9 mph.
1 in 75 rise Beattock to Summit: 2,125 edhp at 47.0 mph.

Table 2 Monday 4th May 1970
16.00 Carlisle and 16.55 Blackpool to Euston
Locomotive: D403
Load: 13 vehicles Mk I stock, 459/485 tons, ETH 47.

m c		m s	speeds
0-00	PRESTON	0.00	–
4-03	Leyland	11.24	30/sigs 8
5-36	Euxton Jn	14.23	46/61
10-32	Coppull Hall Sdgs box	19.32	59
12-78	Boars Head Jn	21.43	76
15-12	WIGAN NORTH WESTERN = 17½	24.33	–
2-49	Bamfurlong	3.40	64/68
5-77	Golborne Jn	6.54	pws 55
8-27	Winwick Jn	9.16	67/73
11-62	WARRINGTON BANK QUAY = 13¼	13.27	–
1-50	Milepost 180½	3.11	41
4-50	Norton Xg	6.04	70
7-49	Weaver Jn box	9.59	pws 14
9-52	Acton Bridge	12.15	60
12-26	Hartford	14.46	69
16-50	Winsford	18.13	76/74
20-73	Coppenhall Jn box	21.36	76/77
24-06	CREWE = 24	26.55	–

Calculated horsepower output:
1 in 135 rise Warrington to MP 180½: 1,795 edhp at 30.6 mph.
77 mph attained on level at Coppenhall: 1,090 edhp if sustained.

Table 3 Sunday 3rd October 1971
11.55 Glasgow to Euston
Locomotives: D413 + D438
Load: 12 vehicles Mk II air-con. stock, 400/430 tons, ETH 59.

m c		m s	speeds
0-00	STOCKPORT	0.00	–
2-28	Cheadle Hulme	3.15	70
4-56	Handforth	5.05	83

Table 3 Continued:

m c		m s	speeds
6-09	Wilmslow	6.02	89
7-59	Alderley Edge	7.07	95/101
10-63	Chelford	8.59	sigs 98/16
14-50	Goostrey	13.01	70
16-43	Holmes Chapel	14.26	89
18-29	Bradwell	15.28	96/99
20-30	Sandbach	17.03	pws 42
24-76	CREWE = 22	24.37	

Net time 22 minutes taking Sandbach slowing as permanent.
Calculated horsepower output:
Average 1 in 600 rise Cheadle Hulme to Alderley Edge: 3,430 edhp at 83.6 mph.
Average 1 in 400 fall Goostrey to Bradwell: 3,390 edhp at 91.5 mph.

Table 4 Wednesday 6th October 1982
07.40 Taunton to Paddington
Locomotive: 50036 *Victorious*
Load: 10 vehicles, 327/330 increasing 340 tons, Mk II air-con. stock, ETH 42.

m c		m s	speeds
0-00	BRISTOL T.M.	0.00	–
1-55	St Annes Park	3.27	56
4-48	Keynsham	6.03	76
7-03	Saltford	7.52	84
9-16	Twerton Tunnels W.	9.24	88/89
11-40	BATH SPA	11.54	–
2-22	Bathampton	3.41	64
5-03	Box	6.02	76/77
7-59	Box Tunnel E.	8.19	66
10-61	Thingley Jn	10.43	86/88
12-74	Chippenham	12.14	85*/pws 77
15-11	Milepost 91¼	13.53	84
19-13	Dauntsey	16.40	88½/89
21-31	Milepost 85½	18.12	82/83
24-01	Wootton Bassett	20.26	sigs 63/10
29-48	Swindon	30.10	59
31-69	Stratton Park	32.07	78
35-29	Shrivenham	34.34	92
40-26	Uffington	37.40	99/100
43-05	Challow	39.20	97/96
46-37	Wantage Road	41.26	99
50-30	Steventon	43.47	101
53-60	Didcot	45.51	sigs 94/98
58-34	Cholsey	48.47	sigs 95/94
62-11	Goring	51.04	100
65-28	Pangbourne	52.59	101/102
68-19	Tilehurst	54.42	sigs 99/41
70-73	READING = 50	58.20	–
2-01	Sonning GF	3.25	sigs/60
4-77	Twyford	5.53	80
8-04	Shottesbrook	8.03	90
11-59	Maidenhead	10.25	97
15-02	Burnham	12.23	100/101
17-43	Slough	13.54	93*/pws 39
19-60	Langley	16.30	48
22-61	West Drayton	19.12	77
25-06	Hayes	20.54	85
30-20	Ealing	24.21	97/98
33-15	Old Oak PSB	26.22	80*
35-73	PADDINGTON = 27¼	30.27	–

*speed restrictions

Calculated horsepower output:
1 in 1,320 rise St Annes Park to Saltford: 1,795 edhp at 72.7 mph.
1 in 660 rise MP 91¼ to MP 86¾: 1,630 edhp at 87.4 mph.
1 in 1,320 fall Shottesbrook to Burnham: 1,560 edhp at 96.6 mph.

Table 5 Saturday 3rd October 1987
14.05 Paddington to Paignton
Locomotive: 50014 *Warspite*
Load: 9 vehicles Mk II air-con. stock, 297/320 tons, ETH 45.

m c			m s	speeds
0-00	PADDINGTON		0.00	–
2-58	Old Oak PSB		4.21	64
5-53	Ealing		6.47	77
10-67	Hayes		10.27	90
14-54	Iver		12.55	97½
18-30	Slough		15.08	100
20-71	Burnham		16.38	100
24-14	Maidenhead		18.39	99
27-69	Shottesbrook		20.53	98
30-76	Twyford		22.48	97
33-72	Sonning GF		24.45	sigs 70
35-73	READING	= 27½	27.59	–
1-63	Southcote Jn		3.01	58
5-25	Theale		5.54	80
8-65	Aldermaston		8.25	87
10-61	Midgham		9.46	88
13-48	Thatcham		11.40	89/sigs
17-10	NEWBURY	= 15½	16.02	–
5-30	Kintbury		6.16	77/80
8-35	Hungerford		8.39	67*
13-26	Bedwyn		11.35	80/81/63*
16-79	Savernake		15.44	66
22-19	Pewsey		19.30	95
25-61	Woodborough		21.39	100
29-12	Milepost 82¼		23.40	102/106
33-63	Lavington		26.24	95*
38-24	Edington		29.06	101 sus
41-39	Heywood Road Jn		31.06	77*/85
47-14	Clink Road Jn		35.24	73*
50-40	Milepost 118		37.52	82/83
53-23	Witham		39.57	81
55-11	Brewham Bridge		41.19	77
58-48	Bruton		43.44	91/96
62-04	Castle Cary		46.07	82*/97
66-75	Keinton Mandeville		49.15	95/94
69-08	Charlton Mackrell		50.37	95/100
72-35	Somerton		52.40	97
74-44	Long Sutton		54.01	93/90
77-58	Curry Rivel Jn		56.05	96
81-55	Athelny		58.32	98
84-70	Cogload Jn box		60.35	86
89-50	TAUNTON		65.47	–
1-77	Norton Fitzwarren		3.20	63
7-08	Wellington		7.47	73/74½
10-69	Whiteball		11.10	62
14-15	Tiverton Parkway		13.41	94/98
15-79	Tiverton Jn		14.49	95/90*
18-15	Cullompton		16.14	92/86
22-33	Hele		19.08	91/98
27-31	Stoke Canon		22.19	87*
30-61	EXETER ST DAVIDS		26.17	–

*speed restrictions

Calculated horsepower output:
Level at Edington: 1,035 edhp at 101 mph sustained.
1 in 86 average rise MP 171 to Whiteball Tunnel: 1,685 edhp at 67 mph.

Table 6 Thursday 29th September 1983
11.38 Plymouth to Manchester
Locomotive: 50011 *Centurion*
Load: 11 vehicles Mk II air-con. stock, 363/370 increasing 375 tons, ETH 49.

Table 6 Continued:

m c			m s	speeds
0-00	PLYMOUTH		0.00	–
1-72	Laira Jn		3.22	56*
4-01	Plympton		5.30	62
6-51	Hemerdon		9.20	30/67
10-63	Ivybridge		13.44	55*/60
14-02	Wrangaton		17.08	57/63
18-39	Rattery		21.40	52*/56
23-09	TOTNES		28.14	–
2-45	Milepost 220¼		4.01	56/*
4-65	Dainton box		6.47	36/57
7-50	Aller Jn box		11.34	pws 18/32
8-59	NEWTON ABBOT	= 12½	16.21	
5-12	Teignmouth		6.19	71/54*
7-78	Dawlish		9.11	63/70
11-50	Starcross		12.34	63*
15-30	Exminster		15.53	77/84
20-14	EXETER ST DAVIDS		20.44	–
3-30	Stoke Canon		4.30	68
8-28	Hele		8.27	82/84
12-46	Cullompton		11.41	70*
14-62	Tiverton Jn		13.31	75
17-52	Milepost 176¼		15.42	78
19-72	Whiteball box		17.34	69/90
23-53	Wellington		20.18	85*/93
30-61	TAUNTON		26.50	–
5-61	Durston		6.03	83/93
11-43	BRIDGWATER		10.51	–
6-24	Highbridge		6.26	84
13-01	Bleadon		10.55	94/96
21-21	Yatton		16.08	93/94
28-48	Milepost 123		20.58	87/90
33-17	BRISTOL T.M.		26.09	–
1-50	Stapleton Road		3.15	46/pws 18
4-00	Milepost 4		7.29	42 att/sigs 0
5-69	BRISTOL PARKWAY	= 9	11.59	–
4-49	Westerleigh Jn		5.48	67/30*
8-66	Rangeworthy		10.13	82/93
12-62	Charfield		12.51	91*/98
17-75	Berkeley Road		16.09	94/98
22-36	Frocester		18.58	95/97
26-01	Standish Jn		21.08	90/96
31-15	Tuffley Jn		24.46	64*
33-16	GLOUCESTER		28.00	–

*speed restrictions

Calculated horsepower output:
1 in 42 rise Plympton to Hemerdon: 2,000 edhp at 40.9 mph.
1 in 115 rise MP 176¼ to Whiteball: 1,685 edhp at 72.3 mph.
1 in 75 rise Stapleton Road to MP 4: 2,080 edhp at 37.4 mph.

Table 7 Saturday 17th September 1988
16.17 Exeter to Waterloo
Locomotive: 50045 *Achilles*
Load: 9 vehicles MkII stock, 288/300 increasing 310 tons, ETH 36.

m c		m s	speeds
0-00	EXETER ST. DAVIDS	0.00	–
0-61	EXETER CENTRAL	2.43	23 max
1-09	Exmouth Jn box	2.11	45
2-66	Pinhoe	3.58	70*
4-56	Broad Clyst	5.35	85/76 min
8-27	WHIMPLE	8.36	

One of the most photographed locations on the WR is at Aller Junction, or Aller Divergence as it is known today, as the actual junction has been repositioned nearer to Newton Abbot. On 20th June 1988 No. 50029 *Renown* takes the Plymouth line at Aller with the 11.59 Portsmouth Harbour-Plymouth service.

CJM

Table 7 Continued:

m c			m s	speeds
1-63	Milepost 161¼		3.05	47/58/pws 20
3-58	FENITON	= 5½	6.41	–
1-28	R. Otter bridge		2.17	63
3-65	Milepost 155½		4.44	59
4-50	HONITON		5.58	–
1-29	Honiton Tunnel W.		2.36	43
4-55	Milepost 150		5.24	92/93/81*
6-72	Seaton Jn		6.53	90/93
10-17	AXMINSTER		9.37	–
2-56	Axe Xg		3.58	61
5.05	Chard Jn		6.01	69/68/75
10-37	Hewish Xg		10.31	71/78
13-09	CREWKERNE		13.15	–
3-45	Hardington		3.51	78/74
6-44	Sutton Bingham		6.09	85/86
8-64	YEOVIL JUNCTION		8.36	–
1-68	Wyke Xg		2.58	57/71
4-44	SHERBORNE		5.47	–
0-64	Milepost 117¼		1.41	41
2-44	Milepost 115½		4.04	45
4-44	Milepost 113½		6.10	63/69
6-08	TEMPLECOMBE		7.58	–
2-16	Milepost 109¾		2.41	72
4-32	Buckhorn Weston Tunnel E.		4.32	67/79
6-58	GILLINGHAM		6.54	–
1-46	Hunts Path Xg		2.43	48
4-05	Semley		5.34	55
6-18	Milepost 99		7.27	80/88
9-04	TISBURY		9.59	–
4-22	Dinton		4.35	84/89
7-14	Milepost 89		6.35	83/84

Table 7 Continued:

m c			m s	speeds
10-03	Wilton South		9.03	42*/58
12-49	SALISBURY		12.17	–
2-25	Milepost 81¼		3.28	58
5-38	Porton		6.21	66
8-02	Amesbury Jn		8.38	70
10-76	Grateley		10.56	83
15-06	Viaduct centre		13.33	102
17-26	ANDOVER		16.04	–
0-59	Milepost 65½		1.32	46
3-59	Milepost 62½		4.45	62
7-10	Whitchurch		7.31	77
10-59	Overton		10.11	83
13-71	Oakley		12.23	89
15-71	Worting Jn		14.03	65*/79
18-39	BASINGSTOKE		16.56	–
5-45	Hook		6.25	sigs 67/59**
11-22	Fleet		11.59	61
14-42	Farnborough		14.43	81
16-60	Milepost 31		16.18	85
19-61	Brookwood		18.16	96/98
23-33	WOKING	= 18½	21.43	–
2-55	West Byfleet		3.18	73
5-15	Weybridge		5.10	83
8-34	Hersham		7.22	93/95
12-23	Surbiton		9.51	92
14-44	New Malden		11.23	74*
17-07	Wimbledon		13.33	59*/68
20-31	Clapham Jn		17.06	sigs 36/63
22-78	Vauxhall		20.44	sigs 15/35
24-22	WATERLOO	= 22¾	24.30	–

* speed restrictions
** possible field divert failure

Calculated horsepower output:
1 in 100 rise R. Otter to MP 155½: 1,750 edhp at 60.3 mph.
1 in 80 rise MP 117¼ to MP 115½: 1,745 edhp at 44.0 mph.
1 in 178 rise MP 65½ to MP 62½: 1,730 edhp at 56.0 mph.
Around 60 mph sustained on level at Fleet: 410 edhp.

Table 8 100 consecutive unchecked climbs of Whiteball bank, 1969 to 1988.
Time and speeds are those between Milepost 171 and tunnelmouth 173m 14c.
Actual rise 1 in 90/86/80 taken as 1 in 86 average.
% column is equivalent drawbar hp over brake hp, without allowing for ETH.
ETH column is maximum figure which may have been drawn for electric heating, in hp.

Date	Train	Origin	Loco(s)	Load/E/F	Time	Speed	EDHP/mph	ETH	%
Class 50 diesel-electrics, taken as 2,700 bhp, all with ETH									
9/12/75	07.30	Paddington	50048	11/360/370	2.04	67/58	2025 at 63	240	75
29/4/76	11.30	Paddington	50011	9/299/315	2.02	66/62	2135 at 64	200	79
9/5/76	08.45	Paddington	50027	9/328/345	3.02	32/48	2100 at 43	200	78
9/10/76	15.30	Paddington	50017	9/306/325	1.46	78/68	2030 at 74	195	75
28/10/76	10.30	Paddington	50041	8/266/275	1.50	75/65	1725 at 71	180	64
30/9/78	10.23	Manchester	50007	11/390/410	2.28	61/45	1435 at 53	240	53
1/10/78	08.30	Paddington	50048	13/433/450	2.19	63/50	1810 at 56	340	67
5/10/78	11.30	Paddington	50018	10/335/360	2.13	67/51	1355 at 59	285	50
27/5/81	12.25	Paddington	50043	9/302/330	1.50	76/64	1755 at 71	255	65
3/10/83	09.20	Liverpool	50008	10/333/360	2.04	71/58	1605 at 63	280	59
6/11/85	09.36	Liverpool	50005	8/268/280	2.06	67/58	1555 at 62	220	58
6/7/86	12.00	Paddington	50036	9/297/320	1.49	77/66	1805 at 72	295	67
8/7/86	11.10	Paddington	50018	9/291/310	1.47	78/66	1765 at 73	235	65
14/9/86	09.45	Paddington	50039	11/366/375	1.57	73/61	1890 at 67	285	70
16/9/86	07.30	Aberdeen	50016	13/432/450	2.12	65/53	1970 at 59	360	73
25/9/86	11.10	Paddington	50032	10/322/335	2.01	72/59	1585 at 65	265	59
27/9/86	12.45	Paddington	50022	11/364/380	2.05	68/56	1800 at 63	325	67
1/9/87	06.45	Swindon	50025	6/213/220	1.38	84/74	1600 at 80	155	59
3/10/87	14.05	Paddington	50014	9/297/320	1.57	73/62	1685 at 67	295	62
Class 52 diesel-hydraulics, taken as 2,760 bhp.									
13/1/69	08.10	Bristol	D1044	7/234/245	2.12	63/56	1440 at 59	–	52
7/6/69	10.00	Scarborough	D1017	9/319/345	1.59	73/63	1875 at 67	–	68
11/6/69	11.30	Paddington	D1020	8/284/305	2.02	71/58	1440 at 64	–	52
11/6/69	17.30	Paddington	D1043	8/276/295	1.58	73/61	1515 at 66	–	55
2/9/69	14.30	Paddington	D1012	10/344/375	2.09	66/54	1730 at 61	–	63
31/5/72	07.30	Paddington	D1026	11/361/375	2.34	59/43	1300 at 51	–	47
5/6/72	09.30	Paddington	D1014	11/361/390	2.19	63/49	1550 at 56	–	56
19/9/72	11.30	Paddington	D1071	9/297/320	1.44	80/69	1920 at 75	–	70
19/6/73	08.00	Bristol	D1009	8/275/285	1.53	74/63	1630 at 69	–	59
18/9/73	15.30	Paddington	D1010	11/360/380	2.17	66/51	1460 at 57	–	53
20/9/73	08.00	Bristol	D1035	8/273/290	1.54	74/63	1630 at 69	–	59
23/9/73	08.45	Paddington	D1047	11/364/380	3.25	33/39	1665 at 38	–	60
24/10/73	07.30	Paddington	D1043	11/362/375	2.24	62/48	1460 at 54	–	53
24/10/73	19.30	Paddington	D1016	11/361/375	2.24	62/48	1460 at 54	–	53
28/10/73	15.30	Paddington	D1067	9/309/330	2.03	70/59	1675 at 64	–	61
30/10/73	07.30	Paddington	D1069	11/361/380	2.14	66/54	1675 at 58	–	61
19/3/74	07.30	Paddington	D1040	10/329/345	2.13	66/55	1620 at 59	–	59
20/3/74	10.30	Paddington	D1055	10/329/340	2.02	71/59	1670 at 64	–	61
30/4/74	07.30	Paddington	D1050	11/362/385	2.13	65/53	1720 at 59	–	62
28/10/74	15.30	Paddington	D1049	11/362/390	2.35	59/43	1320 at 51	–	48
9/3/75	08.45	Paddington	D1028	10/329/345	2.05	68/57	1730 at 63	–	63
16/4/75	13.30	Paddington	D1011	10/329/345	1.58	70/60	1920 at 66	–	70
19/4/75	13.30	Paddington	D1068	11/361/385	2.15	64/52	1700 at 58	–	62
20/4/75	08.45	Paddington	D1067	11/361/380	2.30	58/48	1635 at 52	–	59
23/9/75	15.30	Paddington	D1015	12/396/420	2.37	61/46	1400 at 50	–	51
27/10/75	09.30	Paddington	D1022	10/329/355	2.04	69/57	1700 at 63	–	62
22/3/76	08.00	Bristol	D1030	7/250/260	1.52	76/64	1425 at 70	–	52
13/6/76	08.45	Paddington	D1013	11/360/390	2.19	64/51	1590 at 56	–	58
Class 47 diesel-electrics, taken as derated to 2,580 bhp, Class 47/4 with ETH.									
17/8/70	19.30	Paddington	D1652	9/313/330	1.46	82/67	1560 at 74	–	60
13/6/71	07.30	Bristol	D1696	12/426/435	2.03	69/57	2075 at 64	–	80
15/6/71	06.10	Cardiff	D1594	11/341/365	1.56	73/62	2020 at 68	–	78
4/9/71	10.05	Scarborough	D1535	10/364/385	2.00	71/59	1875 at 65	–	73
8/5/72	07.35	Leeds	D1591	12/440/480	2.08	67/55	2125 at 61	–	82
15/6/76	16.30	Paddington	47171	9/299/315	1.57	73/61	1650 at 67	–	64
9/1/79	08.15	Birmingham	47055	9/314/320	1.51	75/66	2000 at 71	–	78
30/4/79	07.30	Paddington	47477	11/367/385	2.07	67/57	1930 at 62	320	75
15/8/79	07.56	Cardiff	47283	9/309/330	1.53	74/63	1850 at 69	–	72
15/4/80	08.15	Birmingham	47466	10/366/385	2.02	70/57	1775 at 64	210	69
21/1/81	07.56	Cardiff	47121	6/201/210	1.44	79/70	1545 at 75	–	60
12/9/87	07.20	Glasgow	47532	13/432/465	2.14	68/51	1580 at 58	360	61
Class 45 and 46 diesel-electrics, taken as 2,500 bhp, Class 45/1 with ETH.									
4/5/71	06.28	Leeds	D24	9/305/325	1.55	73/62	1855 at 68	–	74
12/6/71	14.30	Leeds	D11	11/376/400	2.02	71/58	1895 at 64	–	76
14/6/71	09.00	Bristol	D113	10/341/345	1.55	73/62	1970 at 68	–	79
16/6/71	13.36	Sheffield	D79	7/247/265	1.57	73/61	1460 at 67	–	58
3/6/72	14.20	Leeds	D70	10/345/370	2.00	71/61	2035 at 65	–	81
6/5/73	19.25	Bristol	D30	12/403/415	2.12	65/53	1945 at 59	–	78
2/4/74	07.41	Leeds	D26	10/346/365	2.03	71/57	1665 at 64	–	67
26/10/74	07.00	Bradford	45015	12/410/440	2.05	69/57	2095 at 63	–	84
10/3/75	06.41	Leeds	45030	8/276/295	2.00	70/60	1715 at 65	–	69
29/4/78	07.00	Bradford	45013	12/394/425	2.07	67/56	2100 at 62	–	84

Date	Train	Origin	Loco(s)	Load/E/F	Time	Speed	EDHP/mph	ETH	%
1/9/79	12.35	Birmingham	45048	9/298/315	2.43	45/49	1930 at 48	–	77
22/9/84	09.20	Manchester	45033	10/364/390	2.03	69/58	1980 at 64	–	79
16/6/71	08.20	Birmingham	D138	10/340/355	2.39	58/42	1260 at 49	–	50
21/10/71	08.20	Birmingham	D186	9/302/310	2.01	70/58	1665 at 65	–	67
14/3/74	08.00	Bristol	46011	7/238/250	1.47	77/68	1780 at 73	–	71
21/4/75	08.00	Cardiff	46009	8/279/290	1.54	75/64	1695 at 69	–	68
31/10/78	07.56	Cardiff	46013	8/276/285	1.50	76/65	1750 at 71	–	70
20/2/79	07.56	Cardiff	46002	8/277/290	1.54	73/62	1720 at 69	–	69
18/7/79	07.56	Cardiff	46016	9/309/330	2.08	67/55	1635 at 61	–	65
12/5/82	07.34	Leeds	45134	11/366/390	2.04	69/58	1955 at 63	320	78
2/3/85	Adex	Walsall	45149	9/296/320	1.58	73/60	1585 at 66	285	63
17/9/85	06.50	Swindon	45110	5/165/170	1.38	84/76	1545 at 80	110	62

Class 42 diesel-hydraulics, taken as 2,304 bhp

Date	Train	Origin	Loco(s)	Load/E/F	Time	Speed	EDHP/mph	ETH	%
30/4/69	14.30	Paddington	D811 + D827	11/384/420	1.44	80/72	2880 at 75	–	63
5/5/69	10.30	Paddington	D819 + D808	9/322/345	1.40	83/75	2550 at 78	–	55
8/6/69	17.30	Paddington	D869 + D822	11/388/425	1.41	84/75	2825 at 78	–	61
9/6/69	10.30	Paddington	D869 + D822	9/326/350	1.37	86/76	2400 at 81	–	52
31/8/71	14.20	Paddington	D812	10/337/355	2.22	62/50	1450 at 55	–	63

Class 43 diesel-hydraulics, taken as 2,200 bhp.

Date	Train	Origin	Loco(s)	Load/E/F	Time	Speed	EDHP/mph	ETH	%
10/5/69	10.10	Bradford	D846	11/385/415	2.44	56/41	1315 at 48	–	60
22/8/70	10.05	Bradford	D861	10/340/365	2.20	63/51	1495 at 56	–	68
4/5/71	19.30	Paddington	D844	9/307/320	2.16	66/49	1130 at 58	–	51

Class 35 diesel-hydraulics, taken as 1,740 bhp.

Date	Train	Origin	Loco(s)	Load/E/F	Time	Speed	EDHP/mph	ETH	%
22/9/73	08.15	Paddington	D7018	7/239/255	2.18	63/51	1110 at 57	–	64

Class 33 diesel-electrics, taken as 1,550 bhp

Date	Train	Origin	Loco(s)	Load/E/F	Time	Speed	EDHP/mph	ETH	%
29/9/83	06.00	Cardiff	33007	4/142/148	1.51	74/66	1110 at 71	90	72

Class 31 diesel-electrics, taken as 1,470 bhp.

Date	Train	Origin	Loco(s)	Load/E/F	Time	Speed	EDHP/mph	ETH	%
20/8/88	10.10	Manchester	31460 + 31450	11/369/400	2.11	66/54	2030 at 60	390	69

Class 20 diesel-electrics, taken as 1,000 bhp.

Date	Train	Origin	Loco(s)	Load/E/F	Time	Speed	EDHP/mph	ETH	%
8/7/84	Railtour charter		20169 + 20184	13/444/480	3.33	47/30	1275 at 37	–	64
8/6/86	Railtour charter		20011 + 20054	9/333/360	3.03	52/37	1185 at 44	–	59
31/8/86	Railtour charter		20094 + 20024	9/333/355	3.58	29/33	1370 at 33	–	69

Class 43/253 High Speed Train diesel-electrics, taken as 2 x 2,250 bhp, all with ETH.

Date	Train	Origin	Loco(s)	Load/E/F	Time	Speed	EDHP/mph	ETH	%
24/9/84	14.45	Paddington	43148 + 43182	7/233/250	1.29	90/87	2515 at 88	325	56
7/7/86	17.45	Paddington	43130 + 43005	8/266/285	1.25	94/88	2510 at 92	365	56
26/9/88	15.50	Paddington	43143 + 43004	8/266/290	1.23	96/89	2445 at 94	365	54

Class 101 DMU, taken as 600 bhp

Date	Train	Origin	Loco(s)	Load/E/F	Time	Speed	EDHP/mph	ETH	%
13/5/84	Relief	Birmingham	Met-Camm	3/89/95	2.21	62/48	–	–	–

Class 155 DMU, taken as 550 bhp.

Date	Train	Origin	Loco(s)	Load/E/F	Time	Speed	EDHP/mph	ETH	%
30/5/88	11.20	Cardiff	Sprinter	2/75/80	1.52	75/64	–	–	–

Although to many the application of Network SouthEast livery to the Class 50 fleet is somewhat garish, when a locomotive and full rake of NSE liveried stock are coupled together the aesthetic appearance is quite pleasing. A full NSE rake, headed by No. 50025 *Invincible* passes Old Oak Common on 13th October 1988 with the 12.00 Oxford-Paddington "Network Express".   *Brian Morrison*

The Refurbishing Programme

Following the BRB's purchase of the fifty Class 50s in the early 1970s, and their redeployment onto the WR, many problems were encountered, with faults ranging from minor electrical malfunctions to serious component failures. In 1973 the BRB, in collaboration with GEC, set out to eradicate the problems, but regrettably, although strict observations were kept on each locomotive, availability figures did not increase.

By 1974-5 the miles per casualty figure had dropped to around 8,500 and during the following 2-3 years, whilst the overall performance had marginally improved, the 1979 WR traction planning was based on an availability figure of just 55%.

Once all fifty locomotives were allocated to the WR the region adopted a 'make simple' maintenance policy where much of the troublesome electronic based systems were isolated, including the Slow Speed Control (SSC) system, rheostatic brakes and automatic wheel slip correction systems. The removal of the rheostatic brake feature did have a minor adverse effect on brake block change periods, which had to be amended to 10-day cycles. With the isolation of the above items, availability did fractionally improve. In 1977 a major initiative by the WR into Class 50 failures was launched which very soon recommended that major modifications/refurbishment of the entire class was necessary if availability figures were to be improved. Such major work, out of the scope of a service/repair depot, would also be very costly and far beyond the normal repair/maintenance budgets.

After authorisation for refurbishing was given, the M&EE Department at the Derby RTC commenced detailed planning together with BREL Doncaster, who were by then responsible for Class 50 overhauls. By early 1978 planning was advanced to a stage where modified electrical equipment was installed in No. 50016. By the end of 1978 refurbishing details were all but finalised and No. 50006, which had been at BREL Doncaster since September 1977, was chosen as the 'refurbishing guinea-pig' but it was not until early 1979 that a start was made on the physical work.

The main areas and operations of the refurbishment programme can be summarised thus:

A. Installation of a new Air Management and primary filtration system, incorporating some 41 filter panels.

B. Modification to Clean Air Compartment (No. 1 end) by the installation of six 'Filterclean' dry pack filter panels in two banks.

C. Major alterations to No. 2 end air filtration compartment including panelling over the former lower roof section and installation of a new angled air filtration system in the position of the former rheostatic brake equipment. The air filters were supplied by Vokes and of similar style to those already used on Class 56 and IC125 power cars.

D. Alteration of compartment layout at No. 2 end with the removal of the engine room circulation bulkhead and the installation of an additional bulkhead between the power unit and generator group to prevent, as much as possible, the air for the generator being contaminated with oil and dirt.

E. Modification to engine room ventilation by the fitting of a scavenger fan and roof extractor to induce the air flow through the No. 1 end side louvre (former window), past the power unit and out via the roof vent. This additional fan was powered by a small motor fed from the auxiliary generator.

F. Elimination of redundant weight transfer equipment.

G. Modification to engine spillage tank and fitting of an 88 gallon capacity retention unit.

H. Full refurbishing of all electrical equipment including re-wiring of all items.

I. Removal of redundant sand equipment and panelling of filler ports.

J. Rewinding of main generator, auxiliary generator and traction motors.

K. Re-routing of previous underfloor cables in new trunking routes.

L. Modification to radiator fan speed control system.

M. Installation of high intensity headlight.

N. Alteration to cab controls to remove all unwanted equipment.

In addition to the above areas, each item of equipment was removed and given a major classified overhaul.

The refurbishing of No. 50006 was something of a nightmare for BREL Doncaster who, to say the least, found themselves working in the dark on equipment totally unfamiliar to them. However much was learned from working on this first locomotive and the refurbishing timescale was considerably trimmed for subsequent machines, indeed the entire refurbishment programme was based on this locomotive.

When the general/refurbish overhaul was first planned the selection of locomotives was to be on the standard maintenance cycle, as locomotives were due main works, but in practice this was not so, with major failures, collisions and general deterioration all dictating the order of arrival.

After arrival at BREL Doncaster, locomotives were first stabled in the yard, where a major inspection was undertaken and any additional body work assessed. At this early stage all fuel, oil and water supplies were drained, with the batteries and fire fighting equipment being removed. The first shop within the works complex visited was the Stripping Shop, where all components including the power unit, generator group, cooler group and bogies were removed, all items being sent to the relevant repair shop.

Whilst in the Stripping Shop de-greasing of all items took place to ensure a clean working atmosphere. Usually some 4-5 days were spent in this shop and when ready to depart body shells were mounted on accommodation bogies for transfer to the Paint Shop. Once at the Paint Shop all interior surfaces were painted, and any external surfaces which were down to bare metal duly treated. On later refurbished examples all original paint on the exterior of the body was removed – using powerful industrial paint stripper, and the body repainted in base green primer. After spending some four days in the Paint Shop the body was transferred to the Main Works 'Crimpsall' building and placed in the No. 4 Bay on works static accommodation stands. The first major operation was the removal of any badly corroded body panels and their replacement with new steel plate. Whilst the steelworkers were operating on the locomotive the former lower roof over the rheostatic brake compartment was plated, any collision damage repaired, the former engine room window at No. 1 end altered to a louvre and the new headlight orifice cut. Once the physical bodywork had been completed the job of reassembly commenced.

The first item to be installed into the shell was the previously assembled main electrical frames at No. 2 end, once these were in situ the job of re-wiring commenced by the works' electricians, an operation which took some 2-3 weeks to complete. With most electrics installed the fully refurbished brake frame was then fitted and a full air/vacuum test effected, using shore supply equipment. This operation included the fitting of the new Vokes air filtration units. After the brake equipment had been refitted the cooling group was re-installed at the No. 1 end. The final item of large equipment to be refitted was the power unit/generator group. After all main items had been replaced there followed a period of connecting up wiring and piping.

At the same time the 'new' driver's desk was fitted and connected up. Once all items had been installed internal cosmetic work was carried out prior to static tests of equipment.

Whilst the body and internal equipment was being dealt with a pair of bogies were prepared in the Bogie Shop. Upon completion of work in 4 Bay (usually about twelve weeks from arrival) the body and bogies were reunited. Once back together as a complete locomotive an inspection followed and after all consumables were replenished the locomotive was started up for the first time, under the watchful eye of the works' test department staff. During the test period each item of the locomotive's equipment, from the performance of the cab heating to the main generator output, was checked and recorded. On average the testing procedures took about one week to complete, if all was satisfactory. If defects were found the locomotive was taken back to the main shop for rectification.

One of the most thorough refurbishing overhauls ever carried out to a diesel-electric class was effected to the Class 50 fleet during the early 1980s at BREL Doncaster. On 9th January 1981, Nos 50012 *Benbow* and 50015 *Valiant* stand side by side in Doncaster Works No. 4 bay during the early stages of refurbishment. *CJM*

After the test department were happy with the static performance of the locomotive it was passed to the Paint Shop where the body work was prepared and repainted, an operation taking some four days. Once the Paint Shop staff were finished a major inspection by both BREL and BR M&EE Inspectors took place which culminated in an active road test, involving hauling a rake of redundant coaching stock vehicles between Doncaster and Newcastle/Peterborough. During the course of this test train operation, inspectors monitored the performance of virtually every technical item and if any defects were detected the locomotive would be returned to the main repair buildings for attention. On some locomotives major faults were identified during the active test period and in some cases resulted in major components such as power units and generators having to be changed.

When the test staff were satisfied that all was correct the locomotive was signed off from the works and released for normal duty. Upon return to the operating department the first job was to despatch the locomotive back to the WR, either by a suitable train service or light engine. Once back on the WR a detailed examination was carried out prior to the locomotive being returned to general traffic. Under the conditions of the refurbishing contract any major problem encountered by the locomotive, for the first few weeks after return to the WR was referred back to BREL Doncaster for attention.

During the refurbishment every item of the locomotive was removed, including all the nose end connections. No. 50028 *Tiger* stands in No. 4 bay at the start of its refurbishment. Note the headlight mounting has yet to be cut, and that the cab section is in base primer. *CJM*

Looking rather forlorn, mounted on works' accommodation stands, No. 50008 *Thunderer* poses inside Doncaster Works No. 4 bay on 21st August 1981, during the early stages of its refurbishment. It was usual practise to leave the locomotive names in situ, until the body was transferred to the paint shop for cosmetic attention. *CJM*

Refurbishing order

TOPS No.	Date on Works	Date work commenced	Date returned to traffic	Notes
50006	29.9.77	21.2.78	13.11.79	Originally called to works for casual repair, reclassified to general/refurbish on 2.1.79.
50003	21.2.79	21.3.79	17.9.80	On works for collision repairs, reclassified to general/refurbish on 1.2.80.
50017	21.6.79	26.7.79	5.2.80	
50019	27.7.79	14.9.79	31.3.80	Called as general and reclassified to general/refurbish on 1.10.79.
50001	29.11.79	30.11.79	9.4.80	
50047	13.12.79	16.12.79	12.5.80	
50020	Called but cancelled due to No. 50013 requiring urgent attention.			
50013	7.1.80	21.1.80	7.6.80	
50023	9.4.80	11.4.80	10.8.80	
50038	25.4.80	2.6.80	12.11.80	Repairs to collision damage also affected.
50004	2.5.80	8.5.80	29.10.80	
50022	28.5.80	11.6.80	19.12.80	
50032	15.8.80	18.8.80	31.11.80	
50015	11.9.80	17.9.80	11.2.81	
50020	14.10.80	15.10.80	6.3.81	
50035	5.11.80	20.11.80	27.3.81	Several failures on test prior to return to traffic.
50012	5.11.80	20.11.80	5.5.81	Power unit change before return to traffic.
50045	Called but cancelled due to No. 50010 requiring urgent attention.			
50010	7.1.81	8.1.81	22.5.81	
50036	2.2.81	9.2.81	18.6.81	
50040	24.2.81	25.2.81	18.7.81	
50045	19.3.81	20.3.81	24.8.81	Prior to returning to traffic, operated to Wolverton Works for Open Day on 22.8.81.
50039	15.4.81	15.4.81	14.9.81	
50033	29.4.81	11.5.81	12.10.81	
50041	29.5.81	1.6.81	29.10.81	
50031	4.6.81	11.6.81	13.11.81	
50008	6.7.81	10.7.81	21.12.81	
50016	10.8.81	14.8.81	16.1.82	
50009	12.9.81	15.9.81	1.2.82	Four weeks late in returning to traffic due to power faults.
50037	30.10.81	4.11.81	6.4.82	
50021	9.11.81	13.11.81	5.4.82	
50044	19.11.81	25.11.81	29.4.82	
50042	6.1.82	11.1.82	22.5.82	
50029	11.1.82	14.1.82	4.6.82	
50025	3.2.82	8.2.82	2.8.82	Delayed due to problems on test.
50005	2.3.82	4.3.82	13.8.82	
50048	5.3.82	23.3.82	2.9.82	
50028	29.3.82	2.4.82	20.10.82	Suffered collision damage at works after completion.
50034	27.5.82	31.5.82	25.10.82	
50024	8.6.82	10.6.82	15.11.82	
50007	Called but cancelled due to No. 50026 requiring urgent attention.			
50026	27.7.82	2.8.82	6.12.82	
50018	6.8.82	12.8.82	20.12.82	
50007	13.9.82	16.9.82	28.2.83	
50046	11.10.82	4.11.82	19.3.83	
50011	22.11.82	26.11.82	15.4.83	
50043	6.12.82	8.12.82	4.5.83	
50049	11.1.83	17.1.83	28.5.83	
50050	17.1.83	26.1.83	5.7.83	
50027	7.2.83	2.3.83	23.7.83	
50030	31.3.83	11.4.83	14.9.83	
50002	31.3.83	25.4.83	20.10.83	
50014	23.5.83	26.5.83	7.12.83	

Sharing works' floor space with a Class 56, No. 50041 *Bulwark,* is seen under refurbishment on 21st August 1981. The duration of time spent inside the main erecting shop was dependent on any body damage or complications incurred during work, but on average locomotives were present for between 10-12 weeks.

CJM

In an advanced stage of refurbishing No. 50001 *Dreadnought* is seen inside No. 4 bay on 29th January 1980. By this time most of the front end equipment had been replaced, new buffers installed, and air/vacuum brake system tests were being carried out.

CJM

After locomotives were completed in the main erecting shop, they were united with a set of bogies and transferred to either the test house or paint shop. Painted in base grey primer No. 50040 *Leviathan* is seen outside the paintshop, in company with one of the works' Class 08 pilots.

Derek Porter

Often accommodation within the paint shop was limited due to other commitments. If this occurred, locomotives were tested within the works before repainting. No. 50035 *Ark Royal* stands in the works yard while brake tests were being carried out. Note the master brake gauge hanging on the cab side window.

Derek Porter

Resplendent in 'more-yellow' livery, No. 50004 *St Vincent* poses in the works yard, adjacent to the weigh shop on 12th October 1980, prior to operating a test train to establish that all equipment was operating correctly. This locomotive was returned to the WR on 26th October. *Derek Porter*

Following the Doncaster refurbishing, the Class 50s were diagrammed to operate back to the WR. A favourite train was the 09.50 Edinburgh-Plymouth onto which the Class 50 was usually attached at York. The upper view, taken on 3rd April 1980 shows No. 50019 *Ramillies* heading away from Chesterfield, while the lower shows No. 50036 *Victorious* near Milford Tunnel, Duffield. *Both Peter Gater*

Operations

by Michael J. Collins BA

Class 50 operations began on 4th September 1967, when No. D400 was released from the English Electric works at Newton-le-Willows. During the 1960s commissioning of new traction did not take a long time, and after static and acceptance trials had been completed, locomotives were soon put into traffic. Only ten days after No. D400 was handed over, the new locomotive was reported hauling an oil train from Dalmarnock to Stanlow. This early working was untypical however, because after delivery the entire class was allocated to Crewe Diesel Depot for duties on the northern section of the West Coast Main Line (WCML).

By January 1968 the first five machines were in traffic, No. D402 was sent to Polmadie for crew training, and No. D404 was similarly engaged operating between Perth and Stirling. Only infrequently did the EE Type 4s work south of Crewe at this time, but Nos D410 and D412 ran to Willesden in October 1968 for tyre turning. One of the first strays from home was on 5th January 1969 when No. D409 worked to Dagenham Dock with an oil train.

Just over a year after the arrival of the first locomotive, the entire fleet was available for traffic. They became a familiar sight on the WCML and branches from Crewe as far north as Inverness. The route with which they were particularly associated however, was on the Crewe-Carlisle-Glasgow main line where their prodigious haulage capabilities were much appreciated by the crews on the long uphill slogs of Shap and Beattock banks. The class put up commendable performances here and were equally at home in control of both passenger and freight traffic.

On 14th April 1968 No. D405 was tried on a number of test trips between Edinburgh and Glasgow, when BR viewed Class 50s as possible traction for the briskly timed shuttles linking the two major Scottish commercial centres. The Class 50 performed very well, but their use was rejected on the grounds that their haulage capability was far too valuable to lose from the WCML. No. D401 paid a brief visit to Toton depot for test purposes on 23rd April 1968, returning to Derby the following day. This locomotive and sister No. D406 were used at the Railway Technical Centre for traction tests. On 25th April 1968 the first serious derailment of a Class 50 occurred, when No. D410 came to grief on the down "Royal Scot" just a mile short of Glasgow Central. It was derailed at a pair of facing points at the north end of Eglington Street station. Polmadie and Eastfield cranes attended, and the locomotive was rerailed the same day.

What is believed to be the first arrival of a Class 50 at Edinburgh Waverley with a service train was on 16th May 1968 when No. D416 arrived at 08.14 on a train from Perth and Inverness. By June, this working began to turn up class members fairly regularly, No. D425 on 7th June and No. D406 on 13th June for example. By the middle of July 1968 Class 50s were working nearly all the regular main line expresses north of Crewe, as well as some parcels trains.

During the period of 'Work to Rule' in early Summer 1968, certain Glasgow and Edinburgh services from the WCML were diverted via the Waverley route. On 28th June 1968 No. D416 worked the 12.05 Euston-Glasgow/Perth via this route, while on 1st July 1968 No. D418 worked the same

train, and on 3rd July No. D400 worked the 14.45 Euston-Glasgow the same way.

Newton Heath depot, Manchester, saw its first visit from a Class 50 on 25th July 1968 when No. D433 received attention. By August of the same year Class 50s were regular visitors to Liverpool Exchange, working the 08.28 from Glasgow to Liverpool and 17.45 return, while another regular diagram was the 11.35 Glasgow-Liverpool.

In September 1968 members of the class began working to Ayr (Falkland Junction) on the 09.49SX freight from Polmadie and the 13.27 return to Bridgeton. Meanwhile, on 14th September 1968, No. D417 arrived at Windermere on an excursion service from Birmingham. This same locomotive was displayed at the Tyseley Open Day held on 29th September 1968. During the autumn of 1968 Class 50s began to appear regularly at Toton for engine testing and tyre-turning. Nos D405/19/21/26/28/29/35 were noted as visitors. On 27th November of that year Nos D400 and D422 worked to Willesden DED for the same purpose. Class members also began to arrive at Tyseley for servicing and tyre turning, in most cases by working revenue earning services to the area. Also, towards the end of 1968 much WCML traffic was being diverted over the Settle and Carlisle line and via Hellifield/Blackburn, especially at weekends. The Class 50s soon became regular performers on these services.

The last Class 50, No. D449, appeared at Glasgow Central for the first time on 12th December 1968 hauling the up "Midday Scot". Later the same month, on 26th December 1968, a glimpse of things to come occurred when the same train was hauled by Nos D405 and D418 working in multiple. It was then widely known that Anglo-Scottish rail traffic was losing out to competition from the airlines. In an attempt to counter this by giving faster point to point timings pending electrification, double-headed Class 50s were introduced on some services over the northern WCML route.

During May 1969 two Class 50s travelled to Darlington to enable bogie rotational tests to be carried out on the surviving Darlington South turntable. The locomotives involved were Nos D405 and D409 on 1st and 27th May respectively.

From the new timetable introduced on 4th May 1970 six daytime WCML workings in each direction between Crewe and Glasgow were scheduled for double-heading using two Class 50s; for this, the entire fleet had multiple control jumpers fitted. In addition to the Euston-Glasgow services, there was a similar working between Preston and Carlisle composed of Liverpool and Manchester portions. At the time many West Coast weekday freights were travelling via the Settle and Carlisle line to ease traffic over Shap, for the benefit of the accelerated expresses and electrification work, with many of these being Class 50 hauled.

On 22nd July 1970 super-power was available for the 10.45 Manchester Victoria-Blackpool when it left for the coast behind No. D448 and Class 40 No. D370 working in tandem.

By 1972, it could be seen that the reign of the Class 50s on WCML services north of Crewe would soon be over. Electrification work was well advanced and engine

Many Class 50 enthusiasts consider that the locomotives were at their best when operating in multiple on the accelerated WCML services between Crewe/Preston and Glasgow. Heading the 14.00 Glasgow-Euston service on 22nd March 1971 Nos D412 and 419 approach Warrington. On the left, electrification masts are already in position. *John Cooper-Smith*

With overhead wires in situ, Class 50 No. 50040 travels at speed near Shap on 2nd April 1974 with a Euston-Carlisle semi-fast service.

Brian Morrison

changing from electric to diesel began to take place further and further north, as the overhead wiring and catenary marched relentlessly towards Scotland. From July 1975 for example, some trains changed engines at Preston and Class 50s were not needed in North West England in such large numbers. At the same time, the Western Region had taken the decision to divest itself of its non-standard diesel-hydraulics. The Class 50s were viewed as an ideal replacement for the powerful Class 52 'Westerns'.

On 11th October 1972 No. D400 was allocated to Bristol Bath Road depot, to be joined shortly after by No. D401. These two locomotives were used for driver and depot staff training which had to take place before the locomotives entered revenue earning service. At the end of 1973 No. D402 headed west with Nos 404 and 411 arriving in early 1974. In March of that year. Nos 50003, D405, 50027 and 50038 followed, (the TOPS renumbering was then in progress), until 35 locomotives were available for the start of the new timetable on 7th May 1974. The WCML electrification was completed at the same time.

The Class 50s were first put to work on the London-Bristol route, whilst the remaining LM allocated locomotives were relegated to secondary duties including much freight working. Transfer of the remaining Class 50s to the WR was complete by May 1976, with the allocation divided between Old Oak Common, Bristol and Laira. By the late 1970s/early 1980s the Class 50s were used on services from Paddington to Oxford, Birmingham, Cheltenham, Bristol, Paignton, Plymouth and Penzance. In the West the Class 50s made

After emigrating south, some of the most scenic views of the Class 50s could be found in the counties of Devon and Cornwall, where the famous sea wall section and the undulating countryside provided some splendid photographic viewpoints. On 23rd August 1986 No. 50040 *Leviathan* pulls round the tight curve at Langstone Rock between Dawlish and Dawlish Warren with the 09.12 Penzance-Paddington.   *CJM*

No. 50008 *Thunderer* pulls a nine-vehicle rake of Mk 2 stock past the NSE station of New Malden on 16th June 1985 with the 08.25 Salisbury to Waterloo.   *CJM*

occasional appearances on freight trains, and with non availability of other motive power they were deployed from time to time on St Blazey based china clay traffic. On Sundays when other traffic levels were low the Class 50s would often be found on engineers' trains, and even during the week were sometimes found on cross-London freight services.

On 3rd March 1980 Nos 50021 and 50024 were tried out in multiple, coupled to a heavy Foster Yeoman stone train between Westbury and Acton. The pair of Class 50s coped successfully with the 3,300 tonne load, but the authorities were not sufficiently impressed to continue with the experiment, preferring to invest in Class 56 traction. Class 50s soon became restricted to selected passenger and parcels duties on the WR, being ousted by IC125 sets on the most prestigious services.

When allocated to the London Midland Region, works responsibility for major repairs rested with BREL Crewe. From January 1977 it was decided to concentrate the majority of repairs to locomotives of English Electric origin at BREL Doncaster. Wherever possible locomotives were worked to Doncaster on service trains. The Class became well known, of course, at the northern end of the East Coast Main Line (ECML) in charge of the works test train and as far south as Peterborough when it became the train destination. When a Class 50 was called to works from Old Oak Common they were often hauled to Temple Mills and then via Cambridge and March to join the ECML at Peterborough. Again, after works visits, BR looked to work the Class 50s back to the WR on revenue earning trains. In the early 1980s the preferred service was the Edinburgh-Plymouth, which a Class 50 would take over at York. From May 1982 this train was operated by IC125 stock and Class 50s were then worked back on any available train. On occasions a resplendent ex-works Class 50 was attached to a freight duty and worked via Birmingham to the West. Sometimes, when Class 50s were on the ER they were used on internal ER duties, such as on 16th June 1987 when No. 50009 was employed on the 08.46 Hull-King's Cross.

Once again, in the closing years of the 1970s the Class 50s were ousted by faster power. Traffic returns on the Bristol main line had been declining because of direct competition with the parallel M4 motorway. It was decided to launch the new High Speed Trains into squadron service on this route in an effort to win back business. The effect of this was to reduce Class 50 appearances on the Bristol main line, except for a time during 1980 when the Class 50s were used to cover for ailing IC125s.

In May 1980 sufficient Class 50s became available from the Bristol route to enable them to be put on the Waterloo-Exeter line, replacing the less powerful Class 33s. This motive power change enabled a significant sharpening up of timings. When there is engineering work between Salisbury and Worting Junction these West of England services are diverted via Southampton and Romsey, thus extending the territory worked by Class 50s on the Waterloo trains.

From the summer timetable of 1981 express services between Paddington and the West of England were recast using IC125 sets. Once again Class 50s were rediagrammed, and began to appear increasingly on West Country inter-regional expresses, which were usually Class 50 worked as far as Birmingham. Occasionally, when there was a shortage of motive power the class worked through to Sheffield or even York. By late 1981 these services were also taken over by IC125s and the Class 50s transferred to other duties. Services to Gloucester and Cheltenham routed via the Cotswold line and the remaining Paddington-Hereford turns became work for the fleet, and by this time the whole class was concentrated at Laira and Old Oak Common depots. A feature of Class 50 work were the Plymouth-Penzance local services, where four or five coaches and an express locomotive were a recipe for some spirited running, despite the many station stops and undulating terrain. During the night of the 14/15th February 1983, No. 50017 operated a car train from Hinksey Yard (Oxford) to Harwich Parkston Quay throughout. The same thing happened four months later on 1st July 1983 when No. 50018 provided the motive power.

The mid 1980s also saw regular workings of the Class to South Wales on selected passenger and parcel services, but by 1987 suitable work for the Class 50s was becoming increasingly difficult to find. This, coupled with high maintenance costs, led to the first withdrawals. The first to be withdrawn was No. 50011, because of its high accumulation of engine hours. Its last working was the 12.15 Penzance-Glasgow parcels on 24th February 1987 which it worked throughout to Crewe, before going to BREL Crewe Works for use as a mobile test bank. By this time works overhauls in the old sense had ended for Class 50s, and under BR's new maintenance policy major depot overhauls were all that remained. Two further Class 50s were withdrawn in 1987 for use as spares to keep the remaining fleet running. The first Class 50 to be broken up was No. 50006 which was sold to Vic Berry of Leicester where it arrived on 8th February 1988. Cutting up commenced soon afterwards, but many parts, including the bogies and windows, were returned to BR for further use. By contrast the first Class 50 to be used on a Royal Train was on 5th May 1987, when green liveried No. 50007 was used on the Southern Region.

Some thought was given to modifying Class 50s for freight work in order to find a new sphere of operation. Accordingly, Laira rebuilt No. 50049 which appeared in Railfreight grey livery, carrying the number 50149. The modified locomotive was initially deployed on test running between Plymouth and Exeter but on Sunday 18th October 1987 was tried on three runs up the steep incline between Westbury and Warminster. In pouring rain the locomotive was evaluated by stopping and starting on the gradient and successfully lifted 22 loaded PGA stone hoppers – a total weight of 1,122 tonnes – up the 1:75 gradient past Dilton Marsh Halt. Despite this, no further conversions were authorised. For over a year No. 50149 fulfilled the role of a Class 37 'stand-in' working china-clay traffic, but was eventually converted back to a standard locomotive for use by Network SouthEast.

The Class 50s have been a popular railtour locomotive for many years. One advantage of a decreasing workload is that a number are spare at weekends and can be made available for special duties. Thus they have made a number of forays into previously uncharted territory, including East Anglia and the South Coast. On 13th April 1985 the pioneer locomotive, No. 50050, visited the Isle of Grain branch with the "Dungeness Pebbledasher" tour. A number too, have appeared at Weymouth on summer dated trains from Bristol, and machines now work regularly from Brighton along the coastway line to Exeter via Southampton and Salisbury. The first locomotive to be seen on this route was No. 50001 on 11th November 1980 when it substituted for a failed Class 33. A number have also appeared at various 'Open Day' events throughout the country, Coalville and Colchester being amongst the more memorable locations.

What then for the future? BR have tried Class 47s on the NSE Waterloo-Exeter route but remained unimpressed, so the Class 50 future is secure on this route for the time being, at least until new traction is introduced.

The instigation of sector pool allocations began to have its effect from May 1989. By this time the Class 50 allocation was concentrated on Old Oak Common and Laira as far as passenger duties were concerned. The Laira machines were used solely on workings on the Waterloo to Exeter axis whilst the London-based machines were concentrated on Thames and Chiltern workings. A few of the more run-down locomotives were working from Bristol Bath Road depot at this time on engineer's department workings. The sad derailment of No.50025 at the hands of mindless vandals occurred on 6th August 1989 at West Ealing and led to its immediate withdrawal. Meanwhile, reliability of the whole class was becoming notoriously bad, the reputation of the Laira-allocated machines being particularly poor. Withdrawal of any Class 50 needing heavy expenditure became a formality. In addition, events elsewhere were having knock-on effects. 'Sprinter' working in Scotland had released sufficient Class 47/7s from Scottish services to make it viable to send some down to Old Oak Common. Also a number of redundant machines from the GE were

sent over to the West London depot. This allowed the NWRA pool of Class 50s (used mainly on Thames and Chiltern lines services) to be reduced. By May 1990, Old Oak Common had received enough Class 47s from else-where to consider ridding itself completely of Class 50s from the Thames and Chiltern services. A few stalwarts hung on until June 1990, even working west on occasions, substituting for ICI25s and Class 47s on summer Saturday trains to Paignton.

The last booked appearance of a Class 50 in the West Midlands occurred on 30th June 1990 when No.50035 worked the 07.18 Paddington-Wolverhampton and balanc-ing return working. Still Class 50s hung on at Old Oak Common, but the end came on 12th July 1990 when all remaining examples (Nos 50023 and 50035) were trans-ferred to Laira for SR duties. This was another nail into the classes' coffin. At the time of writing in Autumn 1990,

Another of the regular stamping grounds for the Class 50 fleet has been the Paddington-Worcester/Hereford route, where their performance has been excellent. On 8th May 1982, No. 50035 *Ark Royal* storms out of Charlbury with the 09.06 Worcester-Paddington. *Brian Beer*

the class are restricted to merely the Waterloo-Salisbury-Exeter services and to Civil Engineer's duties around Bristol/Plymouth. Rumours abound about the future of the class but everyone agrees that the writing is on the wall and that the class will be extinct in months rather than years. Their high maintenance costs are beginning to tell against them.

In September 1990 the decision was taken to replace the Class 50s on the Waterloo-Exeter route with new NSE sponsored Class 159 dmus for introduction in 1992/3. As an interim measure, due to the total unreliability of the Class 50s a revised timetable was introduced from mid January 1991, with some services from Waterloo being replaced with emu or dmu formations. The only work for the engineering department locomotives, allocated to the DCWA sector in the autumn of 1990 were a few duties around Bristol and Exeter, and as soon as Class 37s were available from the Scottish Region, cascaded from the introduction of Class 158 dmus, these will be withdrawn. No doubt the end will be accompanied by sad scenes reminiscent of those dark days when the 'Deltics' eventually succumbed to the inevitable. The Class 50s, with their distinctive sound and powerful appearance, will be missed by all.

Today virtually all workings on weekdays in Cornwall are either formed of multiple unit or High Speed Train stock. In happier days, on 25th April 1987 when locomotive hauled formations were still to be found, No. 50024 *Vanguard* heads a Penzance-Paddington service past Trerulefoot. *Michael J. Collins*

The use of these Class 1 passenger locomotives on Cornish freight traffic has always stimulated great interest, with photographers flocking to the area to capture such workings. No. 50047 *Swiftsure* passes Treviscoe on the Parkandillack branch, with a Parkandillack-St Blazey freight. The train's formation is one VTG van and a rake of the now withdrawn 'Clayhoods'. *Michael J. Collins*

The operation to return the Class 50s to the WR after attention at BREL Doncaster Works caused considerable interest, with the machines often heading Inter-Regional passenger services. On 13th August 1983, No. 50003 *Temeraire* passes Branston, south of Burton with the 14.28 York-Plymouth.

John Tuffs

Since the Class 50s have become popular with enthusiasts, the class have been requested on a number of railtours. Pathfinder Tours "The Suffolkman" which emanated from Bristol, visited East Anglia on 3rd July 1988 and was headed by No. 50022 *Anson*. The train is seen here on the Colchester Down Goods Loop, a very unusual line to be traversed by any passenger train.

Michael J. Collins

Following the failure of Class 50 No. 50025 *Invincible* on a down ballast train in Cornwall on 29th March 1988, Railfreight liveried Class 37 No. 37673 was attached and hauled the complete train into Par. The combination is seen in the down goods loop at Par, while sister No. 50033 *Glorious* passes with the 07.02 Exeter-Penzance.

Michael J. Collins

Maintenance

As with all classes of locomotives, programmed routine maintenance schedules are supplied by the Director of Mechanical & Electrical Engineering to the regional depots. The levels of these examinations are defined by the letters A-F, with examination importance increasing as the letters of the alphabet progress. Each examination corresponds to a number of hours operated by the locomotive and calculated by the Total Operations Processing System (TOPS) computer. It is therefore of paramount importance that accurate reporting of locomotive movements is made to ensure correct maintenance.

Obviously no two locomotives will require the same maintenance, but a guideline as to what work is scheduled is given below.

Maintenance Classifications

A exam – Scheduled for 55 engine hours
B exam – Scheduled for 275 engine hours
C exam – Scheduled for 550 engine hours
D exam – Scheduled for 1,100 engine hours
E exam – Scheduled for 5,000 engine hours
F exam – Scheduled for 10,000 engine hours

A Exam (55 hours)

This exam can be carried out at almost any diesel depot and consists of the fuel, water and coolant levels being checked and topped up as required. All locomotives carry a driver's repair book, this is checked and any problems dealt with. A visual examination of the locomotive is made for any obvious defects.

B Exam (275 hours)

The first of the more important or major examinations is carried out at 275 engine hours, this equating to approximately 3-4 weeks service. Following the usual A exam schedule the items below are dealt with:

Top up engine coolant, check urinal, fill windscreen washer bottle, clean marker lights, headlight and yellow warning ends, inspect and clean cab front and side windows.

The remaining part of the exam is split into two sections: (1) with engine running, (2) with engine stopped. Whilst the engine is running and the inspection staff are outside the locomotive a check is made on the compressor oil level, buffer beam connections, buffers, general condition of body and underframe including doors, roof, battery boxes, electric warning flashes, brake blocks and gear, bogies, AWS receiver, traction motor gearcase lubricating oil level, ETS jumpers and bogies split-pins. With the engine still running, attention passes to the cab where a test of the straight air brake and automatic air and vacuum brake is carried out, this is followed by an AWS test, check of brake pipe pressure, the operation of the driver's safety device, the main reservoir pressure, the operation of windscreen wipers and washers, operation of the hand brake and warning horns. From the cab the inspection transfers to the engine room where engine governor oil level is checked, engine coolant and oil samples taken, whilst the fire fighting equipment, air filters, exhauster oil level, engine oil level and the main fuel filters are checked. The fitting staff now return to the cab and shut down the engine, before moving to the outside of the locomotive to lubricate the bogie movable parts,

Whilst still owned by English Electric Leasings Ltd, and operated by BR, the locomotives were allocated to Crewe Diesel Depot, but also received interim maintenance at Polmadie in Scotland and other NW Division sheds. This view at the south end of Crewe Diesel Depot, on 21st May 1972 shows Nos 423, 430, 405, and 415.
David Percival

handbrake mechanism and buffers. The final part of the examination consists of draining waste oil and checking battery condition.

C Exam (550 hours)
This examination is effected about every 6-8 weeks and consists of all B exam items plus the following:
With the power unit running and staff outside the locomotive a check on the condition of the coupling is made, whilst the bogie lifeguards, hydraulic dampers, wheels and tyres are inspected, as are all traction motor electrical connections. Inside the locomotive the following additional cab items are inspected: anti-slip brake, driver's vigilance device, main reservoir pipe feed pressure. A check is also made on the fire-fighting and safety equipment as well as cab lighting. In the engine room turbo-charger impeller blades, air filters, charge air coolers, engine governor oil level are all checked, as is the radiator unit for satisfactory operation. With the engine shut down attention turns to outside the locomotive where bogies and underframe are thoroughly cleaned and a check made on the condition of the six traction motors and the two air compressors. Returning to the inside of the locomotive body, also with the engine shut down, the radiator elements and engine room floor are cleaned while checks are made to the main generator, auxiliary generator, train heat generator, the radiator

Once on the WR the main stronghold for allocation was Laira depot in Plymouth, where the Class 50s replaced the diesel-hydraulic Class 52s. No. 50005 *Collingwood* stands adjacent to the depot lifting jacks at Laira on 4th December 1987, while being prepared for a lift to change a traction motor. *CJM*

motor, the two traction motor blowers, the two vacuum exhausters, the vacuum limit valve, fuel supply equipment, fuel filtration, engine fuel control linkage and engine exhaust manifolds.

D Exam (1,100 hours)
This level of overhaul is carried out at 1,100 hours, or approximately every 14-16 weeks, again all previous exam operations are repeated plus the following items:
Whilst the engine is in operation the fuel strainer (filler port), air reservoir automatic drain valves are inspected outside the body, whilst the fuel tank is thoroughly cleaned externally. Once inside the locomotive cabs and the usual checks finished, the operation of the DSD holdover button and the illumination of the desk indicators are checked. Inside the engine room the fuel pumps/injectors, air reservoirs and drain valves, low main reservoir protection equipment, air/vacuum proportional valve, turbo-charger, air filters, engine running speed, engine charge air, control air pressure are all checked for satisfactory operation. After the

engine has been shut down additional lubrication of the axle boxes, traction motor suspension bearings and handbrake mechanism is carried out. Still on the outside of the locomotive the brake gear, traction motors and connections, traction motor gear cases, bogie equipment and connections and hydraulic dampers are all overhauled, whilst cleaning of the locomotive underframe and roof is carried out. Inside the locomotive cab the presence of detonator and flag case is checked as is the cab side window operation and doors. After entering the engine room a check is made of fuses, contactors, auxiliary switch equipment and relays, radiator group electrics, fuel supply motor, fuel injectors, engine valve gear and springs, camshaft, exhauster line filters, compressor air supply and secondary air filters are all checked.

E Exam (5,000 hours)

The E exam is now the largest examination carried out on the Class 50s; the E examination is performed by the locomotive's owning depot every 5,000 hours. All previous exam schedules are conformed with plus the following additions:

Whilst the engine is running and outside the locomotive a general examination of body and underframe including doors, roof hatches and battery boxes is carried out. The air reservoir automatic drain valves are also checked for correct operation.

Inside the locomotive engine room the engine governor oil level, air system safety valve, exhauster efficiency, engine running speed, air filters, charge air coolers, control air pressure and water tank low level switch are all given additional maintenance.

After shut down of the power unit all cab doors, windows and movable parts, bogie movable parts, axleboxes, traction motor suspension bearings, handbrake mechanism, drawgear and buffers are lubricated.

Outside the locomotive the compressors, buffer beam equipment, air connections, vacuum pipe, draw gear, buffers, brake gear, traction motor gearcase and bellows, wheels and tyres, AWS receiver, battery condition and nose end jumper connections are all checked.

Back inside the locomotive cab the power controller and master switch unit are thoroughly checked for correct operation. The presence of track circuit operating clips is checked while the cab side window operation, and cab door operation is examined.

Returning to the locomotive engine room, all fuses, contacts, the control cubicle, resistances, radiator group electrics, the vacuum limit valve, the fire protection equipment, EP magnet valves, compressor governor, engine camshaft chain, exhaust manifolds and internal coolant system pipes are all examined.

F Exam (10,000 hours)

The 'F' exam, was carried out every 10,000 hours, and was the largest of the exam categories and consisted of a virtual strip down of the complete locomotive, which would include component changes such as power unit, bogies, generator, etc., if required. The list of jobs carried out at this exam is far too long to list in this book, and indeed the BR maintenance schedule went to more than fifty A4 size pages. As well as changing any defective component the exam called for the complete testing of all equipment including very stringent brake testing. 'F' exams in more recent years could only be effected at Laira depot (on Class 50s) where the locomotives were often out of traffic for anything up to three weeks.

It does, of course, go without saying that if a defective component is found at any maintenance level, the item would be changed. At the time of writing the only depot with a Class 50 allocation is Laira, whose expertise have kept these fine locomotives in service for many years.

The heavy repair shop at Laira consists of two roads, each able to accommodate three locomotives. The two tracks have a central and side walkway to provide a safe working environment for fitting staff. In this view taken on 22nd June 1988 Nos 50027 and 50015 (left), and No. 50005 (right) are seen receiving classified attention, while at the blocks of the track on the right, one of the depot's allocation of Class 43s can be seen.   *CJM*

For many years, until the mid'80s, Laira depot used their M&EE crane to lift Class 50 power units for engine changes. However, following the reclassification of the depot in 1986 to a Level 5 establishment for Class 50 overhauls, (a status which was lost in 1988), a high capacity overhead crane was installed in the entrance of the heavy repair area. With a power unit adjacent, No. 50001 *Dreadnought* stands below the crane in this June 1988 view.
CJM

In the Class 50s' later years the only other depot with an allocation was Old Oak Common, who had responsibility for the NSE fleet used on Paddington-Oxford/Newbury line services. This illustration shows four Class 50s and two Class 47s inside the heavy maintenance factory at Old Oak Common on 26th April 1984.
CJM

A general view outside the seven-track Old Oak Common factory with no fewer than four Class 50s on show. The factory at Old Oak Common was responsible for the classified attention to the depot's allocation, while the day to day running checks and fuelling was carried out in the adjacent fuel point. The locomotive nearest the camera in this illustration is No. 50049 *Defiance*.

CJM

Many Class 50s operating in the West Country visit the stabling and fuel facility adjacent to Exeter St Davids station, occupying the site of the former steam shed. On 14th November 1987 No. 50149 *Defiance* poses in the fuel bay between duties.

CJM

It is not every day that a Class 50 is photographed inside the shed building at Colchester, but on 1st May 1985, No. 50024 *Vanguard* was recorded, being present for the depot's open day.

Ken Brunt

As well as carrying out refurbishment of the Class 50 fleet, BREL Doncaster was responsible for normal classified attention to the class, if one of the regional depots was unable to carry out a repair. Previously refurbished No. 50029 *Renown* is seen in the works No. 4 bay on 7th December 1984 whilst receiving an intermediate overhaul. In the background two Class 31s can be seen.

CJM

Class 50 Names

by J. N. Faulkner MCIT

Warships have several times provided the theme for locomotive names. The LNWR chose a random selection of names from Royal Navy history for its Webb compound 4-4-0s and many of these names were used again by the LMS in the 1930s for its 'Jubilee' class 4-6-0s. When the WR decided to name its Class 42 and 43 diesel-hydraulic locomotives after warships, with a few exceptions, these took their names in alphabetical order from ships past and present. With locomotive naming once again becoming BR policy, the warship theme was chosen in 1978 for the Class 50 diesels. This time the object was to commemorate the British battle fleets of the two world wars. However, names associated with Royalty and the Commonwealth were excluded. Also, as names for the Class 87 electrics had already been chosen appropriately from those of former LNWR and LMS engines, several suitable names were no longer available.

The names for Nos 50001-50013 are those of battleships which served in the 1914 Grand Fleet, commencing with the 1906 revolutionary new design, *Dreadnought*, the only one of these ships not present at the battle of Jutland. The sole survivor to play a part in the Second World War was *Centurion* which was sunk to form a section of a breakwater protecting the Mulberry harbour during the Normandy landings. A notable omission from the class is *Iron Duke*, Jellicoe's flagship, whose name was already carried by Class 87 No. 87017. Soon after the outbreak of the First World War the five 'Queen Elizabeth' class battleships entered service, whose eligible names are carried by Nos 50014-50016. These three ships all took part in the Jutland battle and saw much action in the Second World War; *Warspite* notably at Narvik in 1940 and *Barham* being sunk in the Mediterranean in November 1941. The five 'R' class battleships joined the fleet during 1915-16; of these names *Royal Sovereign* was already carried by electric No. 87002 and others were given to Nos 50017-50020. These ships all served in the Second World War, although *Royal Oak* was torpedoed within Scapa Flow in 1939.

Because of limitations on armaments only two battleships were constructed for the Royal Navy between the two Great Wars; *Rodney* has given its name to No. 50021, but its sister ship, *Nelson* was already covered by No. 87018. The five ships of the 'King George V' class were completed during the Second World War and the two non-Royal names were given to Nos 50022 and 50023. The last battleship to be built for the Royal Navy was *Vanguard*, completed in 1946 whose name was bestowed on No. 50024.

The names of the next seven members of the class belong to that ill-fated type, the battle cruiser. Those of Nos 50025-50028 date from the 1914-18 conflict, when all four fought at Jutland and *Invincible* was sunk, ironically earlier in the war she had taken part in the naval victory off the Falkland Islands. Nos 50029-50031 mark the three battle cruisers launched in 1916-18 which served in the 1939-1945 war. *Repulse* was sunk by Japanese bombers in December 1941, while *Hood* blew up after being hit by the *Bismarck* in May of that year.

The capital ships of today's navy are the aircraft carriers. Nos 50032-50034 take the names of the three carriers converted from battle cruisers during the 1920s; *Courageous* was sunk by a U-boat in the early weeks of the Second World War, while *Glorious* was lost during the Norwegian campaign in 1940. No 50035 refers to one of the most famous naval names, *Ark Royal*, launched in 1937 and sunk in the Mediterranean in 1941, rather than to its post-war successor. Its construction was followed by other fleet carriers which were vital to naval operations during the Second World War and Nos 50036-50039 commemorate these ships. During the later stages of the war a large number of smaller carriers were built, some of which were left incomplete at the return of peace or diverted to other uses; *Bulwark* (No. 50041) thus became a commando carrier. The carrier series concludes with No. 50043 *Eagle*, probably the 1951 vessel, rather than its 1923 predecessor, sunk in 1941.

The Class 50 theme now moves to the three light cruisers which defeated the *Graf Spee* at the Battle of the River Plate in 1939; their names are carried by Nos 50044 *Exeter*, 50045 *Achilles* and 50046 *Ajax*. Finally the choice becomes random for the last four members of the class, Nos 50047-50050. *Swiftsure* is either a 1943 built light cruiser or a 1973 nuclear powered submarine. No. 50048 carries the name *Dauntless* of a 1918 built cruiser which served until 1946 and latterly a shore based training establishment in Berkshire. *Defiance* is not a ship at all, but the name of the torpedo training school at Devonport, once served by Defiance platform, west of Saltash, whose site No. 50049/149 must have passed frequently on its duties in Cornwall. The original member of the class now No. 50050 carries the name of the assault ship *Fearless*, which played a major role in the recapture of the Falkland Islands in the 1980's conflict.

While the concept of the Class 50 names was historic, the practice of the Royal Navy to use traditional names for new vessels has created links between the locomotives and today's ships and their crews, this often being marked by the addition of a commemorative plaque adjacent to the locomotive nameplate. Thus amongst others Nos 50025, 50035 and 50037 are linked to the three aircraft carriers of the present fleet. HMS *Centurion*, the naval pay office at Gosport, originally adopted No. 50011 but when this locomotive was withdrawn in 1987 the name was transferred to No. 50040 the former *Leviathan*. *Leviathan* was one of the carriers left unfinished in 1945!

Nameplate *Warspite*, as carried by No. 50014.   CJM

With the progressive reduction in the members of the Class 50 fleet it is unlikely that No. 50024 *Vanguard* will survive to be twinned with the Navy's first Trident Ballistic Missile submarine of the 1990s.

In 1984 it was decided to name a Class 50 *Sir Edward Elgar*. It was unfortunate that the authorities decided to change the name of No. 50007 *Hercules*, as this has regrettably broken the hitherto sequence of names.

All Class 50 names, with the exception of No.50007 *Sir Edward Elgar,* were of the standard 1970's BR style with red background, being the product of the BREL Foundry at Swindon Works. The plate fitted to No.50007 is non standard and cast in brass. Two background colour changes have occurred over the years. No.50032 *Courageous* was repainted dark blue and No.50149 *Defiance* was painted yellow.

Nameplate *Tiger*, as carried by No. 50028.   *CJM*

Nameplate *Defiance* and crest, as carried by No. 50149. The crest for this locomotive was supplied by the RN Weapons Establishment of the same name, and unveiled in a special ceremony at Laira on 17th July 1988.   *CJM*

Nameplate *Valiant*, as carried by No. 50015.   *CJM*

Builder's plate as fitted to Class 50 No. 50015. These plates, applied either side of the locomotive, were cast in brass, but regrettably, following refurbishment all were removed.   *CJM*

Nameplate *Collingwood*, as carried by No. 50005.   *CJM*

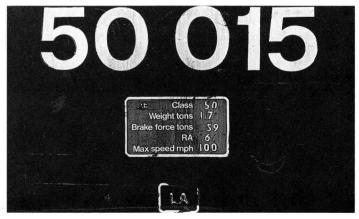

Number area of No. 50015, showing data panel and shed allocation sticker below.   *CJM*

Left: Nameplate *Courageous* and crest, as fitted to No. 50032.
          CJM

A general view of the re-naming ceremony for No. 50007 *Sir Edward Elgar* at Paddington on 25th February 1984. *Barry Edwards*

Since the Class 50 namings, several 'twinning' ceremonies have taken place, where ship or shore establishments have provided twinning shields for application above/below locomotive nameplates. A special ceremony was held at Old Oak Common on 22nd April 1983 when No. 50031 *Hood* was twinned with HMS *Hood*, the specially cast emblems being provided by the Class 50 Locomotive Group. Members of the HMS Hood Association and the Class 50 Locomotive Group stand by the locomotive after the ceremony. *CJM*

Liveries

At the time the EE Type 4, later Class 50 fleet were under construction at Vulcan Foundry, the BRB were in the throes of introducing a 'new' standard livery and their corporate image. By the time the first EE Type 4 was ready for painting the new scheme had been finalised and thus the 50 strong fleet were the first class to be adorned from new in the then new 'BR standard' Rail blue livery. Ends were finished in standard high visibility yellow, while the underframe was painted black as was the buffer beam. In this original condition numbers of the asymmetric style were applied under each cab side window in white, with a corporate style double arrow logo below.

The first major change to the Class 50 livery style came in August 1980, when during the course of refurbishment, No. 50023 was outshopped by BREL Doncaster in 'revised blue' or 'more yellow' livery. This scheme, adopted by BR to try to brighten up the image of its traction was, to say the least, quite startling. The scheme consisted of a Rail blue body, yellow cab ends extending round the body sides to the rear of the cab doors, grey roof – including the formed route indicator box, black window surrounds and red buffer beam. To complete this scheme full height bodyside BR double arrow logos were applied at the No. 2 end and numbers 400mm high applied at the No. 1 end. By the time this scheme was applied the locomotives had all been named, with plates conforming to the standard pattern and were finished with a red ground. Although this livery was adopted as standard for the fleet, several detail differences existed. For example, some locomotives were finished with a black roof and route indicator box area in place of the grey, while one, No. 50010 *Monarch* had the same painted blue.

The most radical departure from BR's previous livery policy came in February 1984, when No. 50007, previously *Hercules*, was selected for renaming *Sir Edward Elgar*, and to coincide with this change of name the locomotive was repainted into mock GWR green livery, which was frowned upon by many enthusiasts.

The application of the green scheme conformed to the style of the original Rail blue of the 1960s. Repainting into green was carried out by contractors at Laira depot. For the first time on a Class 50, the number of No. 50007 was applied on a brass plate to match that of the nameplate.

In the summer of 1986, when southeast director Chris Green decided to relaunch the train services of the London and South East, a new livery was introduced together with a new trading name 'Network SouthEast' (NSE). As the new sector operated some of the Class 50 fleet on their Paddington line duties to Oxford/Newbury, and on the Waterloo –Salisbury/Exeter route the livery was applied to selected Class 50s. On the launch day at Waterloo, No. 50023 *Howe* was used for the official ceremony. The NSE colours consist of a basically blue body with white, red, white and grey bands on the lower levels. On the first locomotives repainted into the scheme the strips turned upwards under the cab side windows and looked a little odd, however on later examples the stripes have been terminated in a diamond shape and the blue colour used has been slightly darkened. All NSE liveried locomotives have black roofs and underframe, yellow cab ends, while the original NSE repaints had white cab window surrounds, later examples having NSE blue window surrounds. For NSE liveried locomotives the nameplates have been slightly lifted to line up between the body side windows, all have a red ground except No. 50032 which is dark blue.

A further twist to the Class 50 liveries came in 1987 when No. 50049 was modified for Railfreight operation, as when complete the locomotive was repainted into the then new Railfreight Speedlink triple grey colour scheme and adorned with the Railfreight red/yellow sector markings on the body sides.

No. 50019 *Ramillies* was repainted out of the NSE scheme, when in the summer of 1989 the locomotive was transferred to the departmental sector and repainted by Laira into all over Rail blue, similar to the original scheme. However a grey roof was added, and slightly larger numbers than standard applied.

In early 1990 a further all over Rail blue example, No.50037 emerged from Laira. However, after only a few weeks the locomotive was reallocated to NSE and repainted in the NSE scheme.

For actual livery details the illustrations included in this section have been selected to show as many detail modifications as possible, including application of numbers and decals.

No. D402 showing the original livery with 'Rail blue' body, full yellow warning ends, and black underframe. Numbers were applied as were logos under all four cab side windows. Note the axle box covers are painted yellow with a red band, and the buffers picked out in silver. *CJM*

No. D402 (with No. 438) showing the 'as-built' livery, with the addition of multiple control jumpers, the heads of which are painted orange.

J. A. Phillips

The first change from standard Rail blue came in August 1980, when No. 50023 *Howe* emerged from refurbishing painted in 'more yellow' livery. This scheme is shown on No. 50033 *Glorious*, seen at Bristol. Some examples in this livery had a black or blue roof applied in place of grey.

CJM

Showing the 1984 applied mock GWR green livery, No. 50007 *Sir Edward Elgar* stands outside Old Oak Common. In addition to its green livery, this locomotive was fitted with cast brass name and number plates and a GWR style logo below the nameplate. *CJM*

The original Network SouthEast livery is shown on No. 50026 *Indomitable*. On this style the bands lifted on the cab sides and to many this spoilt the aesthetic appearance of the livery. Note the revised nameplate position. *CJM*

The revised Network SouthEast livery is shown on No. 50049 *Defiance*. This change to terminating the NSE stripes in the apex of the yellow shaped return of the front end, seems to improve the overall appearance, at the same time the cab window surrounds were painted in NSE blue.

CJM

When No. 50049 was modified by Laira for Railfreight operation and renumbered No. 50149 the locomotive was repainted into Railfreight triple grey livery, and adorned with the Speedlink sector markings. In addition to its grey livery, cast double arrow logos and Laira depot symbol were applied, while the nameplate ground was repainted yellow. No. 50149 is seen at Exeter depot.

CJM

Following the reallocation of No. 50019 *Ramillies* from the NSE sector to Departmental the locomotive was repainted by Laira into all Rail blue livery with full yellow ends, black window surrounds and underframe, together with a mid grey roof. This example was finished with numbers under the driver's side windows, and logo below the windows of the driver's assistant. The nameplates were left in the slightly higher NSE position.

CJM

Departing under the wires from Crewe on 13th August 1968, No. D413 pulls away with the 14.05 Euston-Glasgow. The Class 50 would have replaced a 25kV electric locomotive from this point.
David Wharton

With the front end looking very empty, prior to installation of multiple control jumpers, No. D405 pulls into Carnforth on 1st September 1969 at the head of the 16.15 Windermere-Euston.
John Bird

In addition to working Anglo-Scottish services north of Crewe, the EE Type 4s were used on a number of Blackpool line duties. On 17th July 1969, No. D403 passes Coppull with the 18.20 Blackpool South-Euston.

David Wharton

On 21st June 1969, No. D448 rounds the curve at Elvanfoot near Crawford with train No. 1M37, the 11.22 Perth-Birmingham New Street.

P. W. Robinson

During the final weeks of steam traction on BR in July 1968, Stanier Class 5 No. 45212 stands awaiting departure from Preston with a short freight train, while EE Type 4 No. D425 arrives with the 09.05 Euston to Blackpool and Windermere.

A. Wyn Hobson

Following the introduction of accelerated schedules between Crewe/Preston and Glasgow, pairs of Class 50s became the norm for the express services. On 15th August 1970, Nos D421 and D442 power the 14.00 Glasgow Central-Euston into Preston.

John Faulkner

In common with most classes, following the demise of steam traction the Class 50s lost the 'D' prefix to their numbers. No. 411 is seen arriving at Preston on 15 August 1970 with a Blackpool North-Glasgow service, the train is arriving from the south after travelling via Lostock Hall.

John Faulkner

Before any signs of electrification, track rationalisation or resignalling work had commenced, the 14.05 Euston-Glasgow is seen arriving at Preston in August 1968, headed by locomotives Nos D406 and D449.

John Faulkner

This 1973 view of Preston shows Class 50 No. 404 heading a Mk 2 formation with a WCML service. The overhead live wires were by this time present and the semaphore signalling had given way to multi-aspect colour lights.

M. Norrish

In addition to being rostered to main line passenger duties the EE Type 4 or Class 50s were deployed on selected main line freight duties, including some Freightliner trains. On 21st June 1969, No. D421 is seen near Crawford in the Clyde Valley with the Glasgow-London (Yorkway) containerised freight service.

P. W. Robinson

Before the construction of the obtrusive 25kV overhead power lines, the railway scenery on the LM main line between Weaver Junction and Glasgow offered some superb photographic view points. The 13.00 Euston-Carlisle of 1st June 1970 is viewed at Tebay with No. D425 providing the power.

John Cooper-Smith

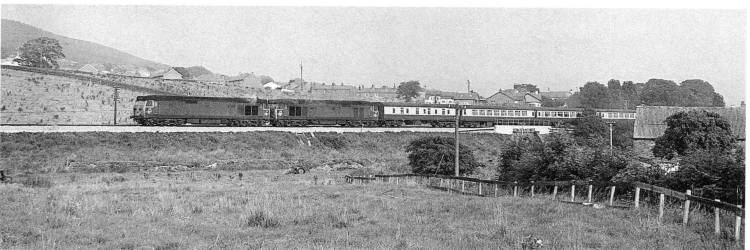

Top: With a new colour light multi-aspect signal in position but still covered, Class 50s Nos 416 and 431 approach Preston on 25th August 1972 with the 11.15 Glasgow-Euston. Both locomotives have their No. 1 end leading. Note the first two panels of grilles on the second locomotive are open.

A. Wyn Hobson

Above: A pair of unidentified Class 50s are seen near Penrith powering the 12.05 Euston-Glasgow Central on 23rd August 1971.

A. Wyn Hobson

Sweeping round the curve at the south end of Penrith, Class 50s Nos 420 and D403 storm through the station with the 12.05 Euston-Glasgow Central on 7th August 1970. When operating in multiple the locomotives were under the control of one driver, who could control the second locomotive via the orange square multi-control equipment.

A. Wyn Hobson

This view of No. 410 passing Maudland Viaduct signal box near Preston on 25th August 1972, with the 11.02 Blackpool North-Euston is dated not only by the presence of a Class 50 on the LM, but by the superb array of period motor vehicles.

A. Wyn Hobson

With a station porter looking to establish where the train's luggage van is located, the 16.00 Glasgow-Euston approaches Carlisle on 16th August 1971, motive power being provided by No. D434. In the bay, a Class 24/1 No. 5125 awaits departure with a vans train to Carlisle.

A. Wyn Hobson

Pioneer member of the Class, No. D400 stands at the head of a Heysham-Euston parcels train at Morecambe Promenade station on 24th May 1968. At this time only 23 locomotives had been released to traffic, and it was unusual to find examples on anything but passenger diagrams.

John Mullard

With 5,400hp at the helm, the 11.20 Glasgow Central-Euston of 19th May 1971 headed by Nos 436 and D428 hurry past Strickland, south of Penrith. When this view was recorded new concrete sleeper track had been laid in readiness for modernisation work.

John Cooper-Smith

Occasionally the Class 50 fleet were diagrammed for Settle & Carlisle line duties. This was usually at the head of freight services, routed from Carlisle to Preston via the S&C and Blackburn. On 22nd August 1975 No. 50031 approaches Dent with a Carlisle-Severn Tunnel Class 7 freight.

John Faulkner

Hednesford on the Rugeley Trent Valley-Cannock and Walsall freight only line, sees little passenger traffic except for diversions. On 20th May 1973 the 08.55 Liverpool Lime Street to Birmingham New Street was one such diversion seen passing Hednesford No. 3 signal box headed by Class 50 No. 402.

Geoff Bannister

Another view of a passenger train on the usually freight only Rugeley to Ryecroft Junction goods line was recorded on 24th February 1974 when No. 432 powered the 08.44 Liverpool Lime Street to Birmingham New Street. This illustration shows the train passing Brereton Sidings signal box at the Rugeley end of the line.

Geoff Bannister

When due to overhead power isolations and 25kV electric locomotives can not operate under their own power, they are often 'dragged' by a diesel locomotive. When allocated to the Midland the Class 50s were frequently used for such duties. On 29th October 1972 No. 437 prepares to detach from Class 86 No. E3128 at Bushbury Junction, Wolverhampton after assisting the 10.39 Manchester Piccadilly-Euston.

Geoff Bannister

Until the late 1970s Class 50 classified maintenance was carried out at BREL Crewe, from where test trains were operated for overhauled locomotives, this usually being to Church Stretton and return. After receiving an intermediate overhaul No. 50033 is seen passing Sutton Bridge Junction, Shrewsbury on 20th April 1974 with the 09.22 Crewe-Church Stretton test train.

Geoff Bannister

Although the Class 50s were built with a Slow Speed Control (SSC) system for operating 'merry go round' principle freight services, the equipment was rarely used. On 8th April 1975 No. 50022 heads the 6K38 Ironbridge CEGB to Trentham, empty mgr train at Cannock Road Junction, Wolverhampton.

Geoff Bannister

On 8th August 1973, No. 408 is seen approaching Cosford station on the Shrewsbury-Wolverhampton line with the 11.05 Ironbridge CEGB to Silverdale Colliery empty mgr train.

Geoff Bannister

No. 50031 with a 'merry go round' coal train from Silverdale to CEGB Ironbridge Power Station crosses the River Severn on the Albert Edward Bridge on 18th August 1975. This bridge was designed by Sir John Fowler and is almost identical to the better known Victoria Bridge on the privately owned Severn Valley Railway.

Andrew Bannister

In the months just prior to reallocation to the WR, Nos 50044 and 50033 pass near the site of the former Shap station on 2nd April 1974 with the 08.30 Glasgow Central-Liverpool.

Brian Morrison

NSE Thames and Chiltern

Following their transfer to the WR, a main area where many Class 50s could be found was around Paddington, where initially they were placed in charge of InterCity services, and in latter days on Network SouthEast and ecs duties. On 27th July 1983 No. 50033 *Glorious* dozes at the buffers at Paddington after arriving with empty coaching stock from Old Oak Common. On the right, sister locomotive No. 50047 *Swiftsure* can be seen. *CJM*

For most of their time on the WR the Class 50s were used extensively on London based commuter services, often with between eight and ten examples arriving/departing during a peak period. On 7th February 1985, No. 50015 *Valiant* awaits to depart from the capital at the head of the 17.30 Paddington-Oxford service.
CJM

Painted in the original style of Network SouthEast livery with angled stripes below the cab windows, No 50017 *Royal Oak*, passes through the washing plant at Kensal Green between Paddington and Old Oak Common on 7th September 1987.

CJM

Heading for the Capital; No. 50032 *Courageous* is seen near Old Oak Common on 15th February 1987 with the 08.30 Exeter St Davids-Paddington. The tall girder bridge in the distance carries the Kensington Olympia-Willesden line over the WR main line.

CJM

Very few Class 50s have ever carried snowploughs, but in recent years it has been the practice to keep at least one locomotive so fitted. No. 50012 *Benbow*, complete with a yellow-painted, 3-section miniature plough passes Acton Poplar Junction on 19th February 1987 with the 12.17 Paddington-Oxford service.
CJM

One of the first Network SouthEast painted "Hoovers" No. 50023 *Howe*, is seen between Ealing Broadway and Acton on 7th July 1986 with the 09.03 Oxford-Paddington. At this time although the route was operated by NSE, very few coaching stock vehicles were painted in the sector colours.

CJM

Following the introduction of Mk 3 sleeper stock on the WR Paddington-Penzance route, Old Oak Common ceased to be responsible for maintenance, which was transferred to Wembley IC depot. To transfer stock from Paddington to Wembley the ecs was routed via the Greenford Loop, and Acton Wells Junction to Willesden. On 18th February 1987 the stock transfer was headed by No. 50039 *Implacable* and is seen near Ealing Broadway.
CJM

Hauling an interesting array of different designed Mk 2 stock, NSE liveried No. 50037 *Illustrious* travels over the up slow line at West Ealing with the 10.11 Birmingham-Paddington working on 23rd February 1987.

CJM

The use of Class 50s on non-passenger duties in the London area is quite rare, even more so when the train is captured pulling off the Greenford loop line at West Ealing! This illustration, taken on 12th April 1984, shows No. 50020 *Revenge* heading a short engineers' special bound for Old Oak Common.

John Faulkner

With a complete rake of Network SouthEast liveried Mk 1 stock behind, 'more yellow' No. 50012 *Benbow*, complete with snowploughs passes West Drayton on 28th November 1987 with the 12.00 Oxford-Paddington ''Network Express''.

CJM

In pristine condition, No. 50032 *Courageous* storms past the industrial complex between Slough and Langley on 6th November 1986 with the 11.10 Oxford-Paddington. This section of the four-track GW main line offers some very pleasant photographic locations.

CJM

With the Windsor line branch diverging in the left foreground, Class 50 No. 50018 *Resolution* hurries past Slough with the 11.05 Oxford-Paddington diagram on 8th January 1983. The Paddington-Oxford NSE service was one of the last remaining loco/stock operated routes, and was taken over by Class 47s in mid 1990.

Alex Dasi-Sutton

The 2,700hp available from the Class 50 is slightly over kill for this very light weight automotive train conveying just nine lorry cab units. The train which originated from BL Cowley is headed by No. 50045 *Achilles* and is seen passing Taplow on 3rd September 1984.

John Stretton

During the late 1980s, photographers looking for Class 50 activity were well advised to make their photographic forays in the Reading-London area where, if one was lucky up to 20 movements could be recorded in a day. On 16th February 1987 No. 50034 *Furious* hurries through Sonning Cutting at the head of the 10.11 Birmingham-Paddington.

CJM

The hourly interval "Network Express" service from Paddington to Oxford was, during the late 1980s, operated by either Class 47 or 50 locomotives, and offered photographers, especially in the photogenic Thames Valley between Reading and Didcot, much potential. Traversing the up slow line at Lower Basildon on 5th August 1987 No. 50022 *Anson* heads the 14.46 ecs from Oxford to Old Oak Common formed mostly of NSE liveried Mk 2 stock.

CJM

The Old Oak Common allocation of Class 50s were always maintained in a very clean external condition. With remains of silver painted buffers still evident and axle boxes picked out in yellow, No. 50036 *Victorious* approaches Oxford on 10th August 1987 with the 14.17 departure from Paddington.

Alex Dasi-Sutton

In the short period of the Class 50s operation on the WR before naming was introduced, two examples are seen passing at Reading on 6th March 1977. No. 50013 departs from the station with the 08.35 Penzance-Paddington, while sister No. 50027 approaches with the 13.30 Paddington-Penzance.

Les Bertram

Approaching Didcot on the down slow line, passing Moreton, No. 50036 *Victorious* hauls the 15.15 Paddington-Oxford "Network Express" service on 3rd June 1989. Although this locomotive did not carry NSE livery, it was operated by the Network Thames & Chiltern sector.
CJM

During the final weeks of use on the NSE Paddington-Oxford route, No.50023 *Howe* stops at Reading on 5th July 1990 with the 16.00 Oxford-Paddington 'Network Express'.
CJM

The much followed Class 50s replaced the Class 33s on the Waterloo-Exeter route from May 1980, and have produced some very lively running. Photographed from the site of the old Nine Elms shed on 31st August 1987, the 12.10 Waterloo-Exeter St Davids is headed by No. 50008 *Thunderer*, while on the down Windsor line is an eight-car formation of Class 455 stock.
Brian Morrison

Twelve miles from Waterloo, and half way to the first scheduled stop at Woking, is Surbiton, where on 17th April 1981 the 15.10 Waterloo-Exeter St Davids passes, headed by No. 50028 *Tiger*.
CJM

West of Woking is Woking Junction where the Guildford and Basingstoke lines diverge, the main Basingstoke-West of England route then passes through the photogenic St Johns Cutting between Woking Junction and Brookwood, from where No. 50027 *Lion* emerges into the sunshine at Woking Junction on 18th October 1987 with the 08.18 Exeter-Waterloo.

CJM

With the Basingstoke Canal to the right, No. 50008 *Thunderer* heads for Pirbright Junction on 10th April 1987 with the 08.11 Exeter St Davids-Waterloo. This Class 50 is one of several that have carried naval twinning plates near to the nameplates.

CJM

Pulling through the quadruple bored aqueduct carrying the Basingstoke Canal over the LSWR main line between Brookwood and Farnborough, No. 50005 *Collingwood* hauls the 13.10 Waterloo-Exeter St Davids on 10th April 1987.

CJM

Before its repaint into mock GW green livery and being renamed *Sir Edward Elgar*, No. 50007 *Hercules* approaches Hook on 3rd August 1983 with the 12.25 Exeter St Davids-Waterloo service.

CJM

In days prior to refurbishment, and when full buffet car facilities were provided on the Waterloo-West of England route, the 06.15 Exeter St Davids-Waterloo passes near the village of Basing powered by No. 50050 *Fearless*. On the down line an SR 4REP/8TC formation is seen on a Waterloo-Bournemouth service, 15th April 1980.

CJM

Photographed during the period of livery transition from blue/grey to Network SouthEast, the 09.38 Exeter St Davids-Waterloo on 23rd April 1987 is seen on the outskirts of Basingstoke headed by No. 50010 *Monarch*. These services usually traverse the up main line, but due to an engineering occupation the train is using the slow line. *CJM*

From Worting Junction, west of Basingstoke the West of England route continues, at present unelectrified, however finance will be sought to continue the 3rd rail electrification onto Salisbury in the future. Passing the site of the closed Oakley station on 23rd April 1987 the 12.20 Exeter St Davids-Waterloo is seen powered by No. 50013 *Agincourt*. *CJM*

Between Basingstoke and Salisbury, the three smaller stations of Overton, Whitchurch and Grateley are not served by many West of England expresses, an oversight as most areas now have sizeable residential areas. Racing past Whitchurch on 13th April 1984 the 09.38 Exeter St Davids-Waterloo duty is headed by the ever popular No. 50008 *Thunderer*. *CJM*

After a covering of overnight snow, the 12.20 Exeter St Davids-Waterloo with No. 50050 *Fearless* at the helm hurries past Grateley on 15th January 1985. It is in weather conditions such as this that the non-electrified routes of the SR fare slightly better, as there is no live rail to freeze up! *CJM*

A popular area for railway photographers is around Salisbury, as in addition to the West of England route the cross country line between Westbury and Southampton passes through, which brings an amount of freight traffic to the city. Approaching the station from Tunnel Junction on 13th June 1986 No. 50019 *Ramillies* hauls the 11.10 Waterloo-Exeter St Davids.

Alex Dasi-Sutton

After departure from Salisbury the LSWR route traverses some very nice countryside, especially in the area around Tisbury. On 18th October 1986 the 09.38 Exeter St Davids-Waterloo is seen near Tisbury with No. 50010 *Monarch* in charge.

Brian Morrison

It is unfortunate that much of the LSWR West of England route is now of single track, as this considerably restricts the number of movements possible. Passing the village of Wilmington near Honiton, No. 50001 *Dreadnought* powers the 13.10 Waterloo-Exeter St Davids on 21st April 1987.

CJM

By 1989 it was rare to capture any non-passenger train on the LSWR route to the west, however on 4th July 1989 this superb view of No. 50004 *St Vincent* was captured on an engineers' train entering Honiton station.

Reg Jones

Displaying its NSE livery, No. 50049 *Defiance* is seen passing Whitford near Seaton Junction on 4th July 1989 with the 11.15 Waterloo-Exeter St Davids service.

Reg Jones

On the double track section, west of Pinhoe, approaching Exmouth Junction, No. 50010 *Monarch* powers the 09.10 service from Waterloo on 5th October 1984. In the distance adjacent to the fourth coach of the train, an up service can be seen slowly approaching Pinhoe and the entrance to the single line to Honiton.

CJM

With its body glowing after a recent repaint at Laira, No. 50007 *Sir Edward Elgar* departs from Exeter Central on 16th July 1989 with the 09.28 Exeter St Davids–Waterloo. Following the transfer of No. 50007 to the NSE fleet in Spring 1989 many followers thought that the locomotive might be repainted into Network colours, but thankfully this was not the case.

Reg Jones

If due to engineering work the route west of Woking is blocked, it is not uncommon for the West of England services to be routed via Guildford, the Portsmouth direct line and Southampton to reach Salisbury. This does of course add to the already long journey time. On 28th February 1987 the 09.10 Waterloo-Exeter St Davids is seen approaching Guildford behind No. 50015 *Valiant*.

Alex Dasi-Sutton

On the same day as the previous illustration was taken, the 11.10 Waterloo-Exeter St Davids is seen approaching Farlington Junction near Havant with No. 50020 *Revenge* at the front. By the number of faces peering from the windows of the leading two coaches it would appear that a number of Class 50 'bashers' were on board.   *Alex Dasi-Sutton*

For two years, between May 1987 and May 1989, a Class 50 was rostered each day to operate one service each way between Waterloo and Portsmouth Harbour. This was to provide a Class 50 and stock in the Hampshire City for the daily Portsmouth-Plymouth service. On 3rd January 1989 No. 50017 *Royal Oak*, pulls off the Guildford line at Havant with the 09.22 Waterloo-Portsmouth Harbour.   *Brian Morrison*

Displaying the later revised Network livery, No. 50028 *Tiger* passes Cosham with the 09.33 Plymouth-Portsmouth Harbour diagram on 3rd January 1989. From the commencement of the May 1989 timetable this service was withdrawn, with passengers from the West of England for Portsmouth having to change at Salisbury.

Brian Morrison

On 28th February 1984, line possessions dictated that the Waterloo-Exeter service be routed from Worting Junction to Salisbury via Eastleigh and Southampton. The down 09.10 service of the day is seen passing Eastleigh with No. 50025 *Invincible* providing the power.

Alex Dasi-Sutton

When the majority of Paddington-West of England services were in the hands of Class 50s, one of the most popular photographic haunts was on the Berks & Hants line between Reading West and Westbury. The 08.34 Penzance-Paddington service of 4th March 1980, headed by No. 50018 *Resolution* passes the housing estates on the outskirts of Reading at Southcoat Junction.

CJM

The same locomotive as in the previous illustration, No. 50018, but now refurbished and painted in 'more yellow' livery is seen near Midgham on 8th July 1986 heading the 11.10 Paddington-Paignton "Torbay Express" service.

CJM

Before BR lost the contract to move the bulk of newspapers from the major printing cities in the summer of 1988, there was one van train per day on the B&H line conveying empty vans from Plymouth to Old Oak Common. On 19th March 1987 motive power was provided by No. 50010 *Monarch*, this view was taken at Old Mill near Aldermaston.

CJM

For much of its length the Berks & Hants line has the very pleasant Kennet & Avon Canal running parallel. This view at Hungerford Common on 8th July 1986 shows No. 50023 *Howe* hauling the 10.00 Paignton-Paddington. The canal can be seen on the right, while the station is in the far distance.

CJM

The western end of the Berks & Hants line is at Westbury, where trains can either travel via Westbury or the Westbury avoiding line. In the shadow of the famous Westbury White Horse, No. 50007 *Sir Edward Elgar* heads towards Fairwood Junction on 23rd October 1984 with the 13.40 Paddington-Penzance.

CJM

A typical scene on the West Coast Main Line during the early 1970s, showing a pair of Class 50s at the head of an express passenger formation. On 9th September 1972 Nos D434 and D424 pass Shap Wells with the 14.00 Euston-Glasgow. *John Cooper-Smith*

No. 50022 *Anson* pulls into Truro on 11th September 1978 with the up "Cornish Riviera Express" from Penzance to Paddington. The warehouse in the background occupies the site of the former locomotive depot. *CJM*

No. 50026 *Indomitable* hurries past the clay driers at Burngullow on 11th September 1978 with the 07.30 Paddington-Penzance. The Class 50s were used on Paddington-West of England expresses after the demise of diesel hydraulic power and prior to the introduction of IC125s.
CJM

In beautiful evening sunshine No. 50032 *Courageous* slows for the station stop at Par on 3rd October 1984 whilst in charge of the 16.35 Plymouth-Penzance local.
CJM

No. 50038 *Formidable* climbs Dainton Bank with a Paddington-Penzance working on 20th July 1985.

No. 50043 *Eagle* passes Old Mill, Aldermaston on 8th July 1986 with a Plymouth-Old Oak Common van train. *CJM*

Inset Right: Passing the former junction for the Kingsbridge line at Brent, No. 50028 *Tiger* passes the remains of the station on 2nd July 1984 with the 10.24 Penzance-Liverpool service. The locomotive would have worked this train as far as Birmingham New Street.   *CJM*

Inset below: Pulling off the single line section of the former LSWR main line at Honiton, No. 50037 *Illustrious* slows for the station stop with the 13.10 Waterloo-Exeter St Davids service on 4th July 1984.   *CJM*

Main picture: Even after IC125s had taken over the majority of West of England duties, Class 50s could still be found on the route, especially at weekends. On 21st June 1981 the 13.30 Paignton-Paddington passes Worth, to the east of Exeter with No. 50046 *Ajax* at the head.
CJM

Inset below: The setting of Cowley Bridge Junction near Exeter, where the Barnstaple line joins the main Western arterial route, provides an interesting photographic viewpoint. No. 50022 *Anson* approaches the junction on 6th July 1984 with the 13.40 Paddington-Penzance service.
CJM

After traversing the bank of the River Teign from Newton Abbot, No. 50009 *Conqueror* rounds the curve at Shaldon Bridge near Teignmouth Docks on 20th April 1987, while in charge of the 07.30 Penzance-Glasgow service.   *CJM*

Network SouthEast liveried No. 50034 *Furious* pulls away from Exeter Central towards Exeter St James Park on 7th July 1987 with the 09.38 Exeter-Waterloo working.   *CJM*

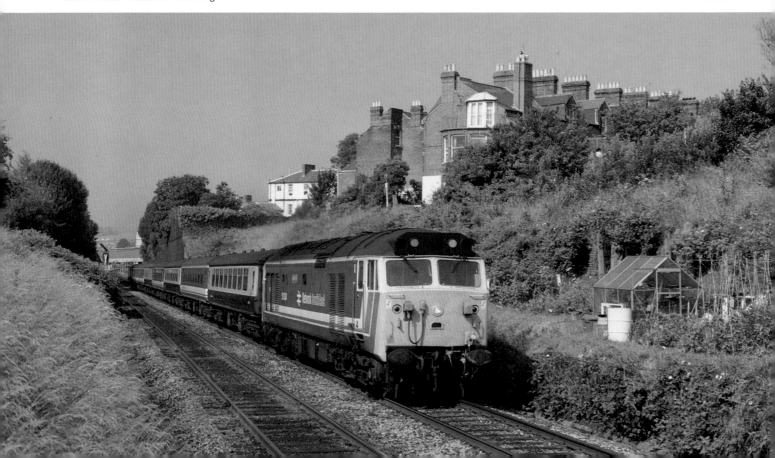

In early Network SouthEast livery, No. 50029 *Renown* approaches Aller divergence, west of Newton Abbot on 26th August 1987 with the 11.45 Paddington-Penzance.

CJM

No. 50018 *Resolution* approaches New Malden on the SR route to the West on 29th May 1989, while in charge of the 13.15 Waterloo-Exeter.

Jeremy de Souza

No. 50007 *Sir Edward Elgar*, in distinctive green livery, climbs towards Dainton summit with an up civil engineers' train conveying continuous welded rail empties, bound for Exeter on 21st April 1987.
Michael J. Collins

In 1989, as a result of the implementation of sector ownership, many locomotives appeared in revised liveries. No. 50019 *Ramillies*, formerly in Network SouthEast colours, was repainted by Laira in all-over rail blue following the transfer of the locomotive to the Departmental fleet. No. 50019 is seen here at Merehead on 25th June 1989 when it took part in the Foster Yeoman rail event.
CJM

No. 50012 *Benbow* storms away from the western portal of Somerton Tunnel between Castle Cary and Cogload on 11th September 1985, while in charge of the 13.40 Paddington-Penzance.

Steve Smithee

The section of line between Cogload Junction and Taunton was, until the mid 1980s, of four-track layout, but alas today only two lines remain. With four tracks still in situ at Cogload on 28th March 1985 two Class 50 hauled services pass; on the up line (towards camera) No. 50005 *Collingwood* heads the 09.32 Penzance-Paddington while on the down No. 50013 *Agincourt* hauls the 09.36 Liverpool Lime Street-Penzance.

Brian Morrison

The area around Taunton is today only a mere shadow of its former self, with the approaches being virtually of one up and one down line. When the goods loops (left) were still present, No. 50043 *Eagle* departs from the station with the 07.30 Penzance-Glasgow on 28th March 1985.   *CJM*

Approaching a gantry that once supported an abundance of semaphore signals, No. 50040 *Leviathan* passes Silk Mill Crossing west of Taunton with the 09.23 Newcastle-Penzance on 31st March 1986. The two surviving gantry signals and the two post mounted signals in the CCE yard were in the throes of being removed when this illustration was taken.   *Michael J. Collins*

No. 50047 *Swiftsure*, one of the first examples to be withdrawn, approaches Taunton from Silk Mill Crossing under a somewhat stormy sky on 28th March 1985 with the 06.15 Plymouth-Old Oak Common vans.

CJM

Sporting the last two digits of its number above the headlight No. 50035 *Ark Royal* waits in the loop at Bathampton on 7th May 1988 while in charge of the 13.44 Bristol Temple Meads-Paddington parcels service. Hurrying past on the main line, InterCity 125 set No. 253045 forms the 13.10 Weston-Super-Mare-Paddington.

Michael J. Collins

Displaying its departmental CCE livery of all over rail blue with full yellow ends, No. 50019 *Ramillies* passes Oldfield Park, Bath on 14th May 1989 in charge of an engineers' ballast train.

John Chalcraft

Passing the site of the now defunct Winterbourne station, closed to passengers from April 1961, Class 50 No. 50009 *Conqueror* hauls the 07.35 Plymouth-Birmingham New Street towards Westerleigh Junction in the summer of 1985. From Westerleigh Junction this train was routed via Gloucester and Cheltenham.

CJM

A short premium parcels train from Bristol Temple Meads to Paddington formed of just four vans, approaches Saltford on 16th March 1988 headed by No. 50038 *Formidable*. Looking at this picture one would not think it was taken only seven miles from the centre of Bristol.

CJM

Often the trackside viewpoint can give some of the most impressive pictures, this low elevation shot at Marlands, at the northern portal of Whiteball Tunnel shows No. 50039 *Implacable* heading the 09.32 Penzance-Paddington on 25th September 1985.

Steve Smithee

Devonshire Workings

In all over Rail blue livery, with full yellow warning ends No. 50043 *Eagle* passes Worth near Tiverton on 14th June 1981 while in charge of the 11.25 Paddington-Plymouth. In the late 1970s/early 1980s virtually all West of England services were hauled by Class 50s, replacing the 'Western' Class 52s in 1977.

CJM

When the M5 motorway was built as far west as Exeter it followed the Taunton-Exeter railway line for much of the way, and in places this provided additional vantage points from which to photograph trains while in others it totally spoilt the view. Near Cullompton on 21st June 1981 the 10.30 Liverpool-Plymouth service passes Junction 28 on the M5, headed by No. 50038 *Formidable*.

Jean Marsden

Without any possible doubt, the most photographed section of the West of England main line must be along the sea wall section between Starcross and Teignmouth. With a freight consist including the now withdrawn clay hood wagons, No. 50039 *Implacable* passes Dawlish Warren on 19th June 1980 with a Gloucester-Plymouth Friary working.

CJM

With the ever-popular seaside town of Dawlish in the background, No. 50039 *Implacable* rounds the tight left curve at Langstone Rock between Dawlish and Dawlish Warren with the 11.20 Paignton-Paddington on 23rd August 1983. Thankfully even in their demise the Class 50s were still a frequent sight along the sea wall section.

CJM

Fortunately being a resident of Dawlish the author has the chance to wait for good weather to capture trains on the sea wall. In almost perfect conditions, snowplough-fitted No. 50018 *Resolution* hauls one of the final workings of the up 06.15 Plymouth-Paddington vans on 2nd July 1988 past the 'Rockstone' bridge near Dawlish. All views of the wall are considerably enhanced by the tide being in.
CJM

Not the weather for sunbathers! On 11th September 1988 the rough sea almost prevented trains from running along the sea wall at Dawlish due to interference with the modern colour light signalling equipment. Braving the storm No. 50009 *Conqueror* slowly travels west with an engineers' special from Taunton to Plymouth.

CJM

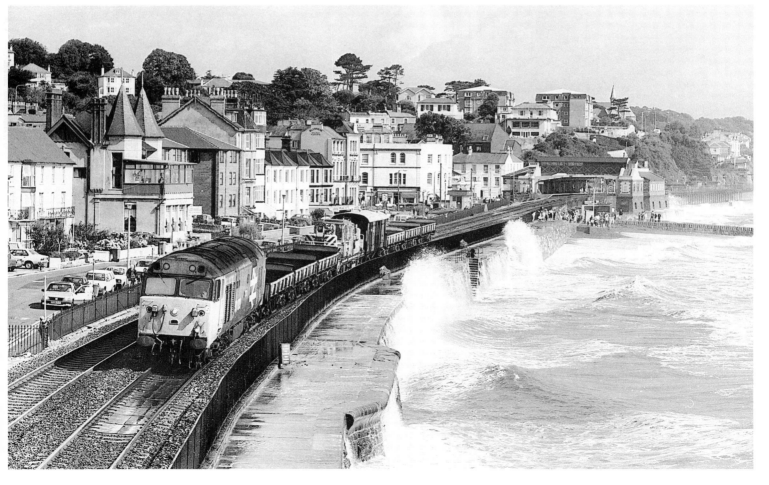

All-blue liveried No.50019 *Ramillies* passes slowly along the sea wall at Dawlish with two wagons of track sections on 4th March 1990 forming a civil engineers' special from Exeter Riverside to Tavistock Junction. *CJM*

As well as at Dawlish, the sea wall, ideal for rail observations, continues along the coastal edge between Holcombe and Teignmouth. With St Michaels church, Teignmouth in the distance, No. 50029 *Renown* pulls along the Teignmouth wall on 30th January 1989 with the 09.40 Plymouth-Portsmouth Harbour. *CJM*

This superb signal gantry at Newton Abbot, although removed from BR use can still be seen, as it is now preserved in the car park of publishers David & Charles adjacent to the station. Hauling the now-withdrawn 07.58 Paddington-St Austell Motorail service under the gantry on 17th September 1982 is No. 50032 *Courageous*. It is no wonder that this service was withdrawn when the loading of this train is taken into account! *CJM*

To the west of Newton Abbot lies Aller Junction, the diverging point for the Paignton line from the main route to Plymouth. Approaching the junction from the Plymouth line on 14th September 1982 No. 50029 *Renown* heads the 07.40 Penzance-Liverpool, while in the distance an InterCity 125 can be seen disappearing towards Dainton.

CJM

Although Aller Junction is still referred to as such, since the track modernisation of the mid-1980s, the actual junction is near Newton Abbot and only the divergence still exists at Aller. Pulling off the Paignton line on 2nd September 1990, No.50017 *Royal Oak* heads the 17.35 Paignton-Waterloo.

CJM

With a few remains of the former down goods loop still evident at Aller Junction, the 07.40 Kensington Olympia-St Austell Motorail service of 27th June 1981 applies power for the arduous climb of Dainton bank, with all blue refurbished No. 50017 *Royal Oak* at the helm.
CJM

Today only one station survives between Newton Abbot and Plymouth, that of Totnes, which for a few years in the 1980s had the pleasure of the Dart Valley Railway steam service running into its platforms on selected days. On 20th April 1987, Class 50 No. 50006 *Neptune* passes through the station on the middle road with the 10.00 Penzance-Paddington, while ex-GWR 4500 class 2-6-2T No.4555 stands in the up platform waiting to run round before returning to Buckfastleigh.
CJM

Running down grade from Tigley, on Rattery bank, Network SouthEast liveried No. 50019 *Ramillies* slows for the station pointwork at Totnes on 3rd November 1988 with the 09.40 Plymouth-Portsmouth Harbour service. *CJM*

Since their introduction on the WR, the Class 50s have been widely used on departmental and engineering duties, where perhaps their 2,700hp is somewhat wasted. On 3rd May 1983 No. 50038 *Formidable* meanders through the Devon countryside near Totnes with an empty ballast train from Tavistock Junction to Meldon Quarry. *CJM*

The first gruelling incline for trains heading east out of Plymouth is Hemerdon bank, five miles from North Road station, with a rise of 1 in 42. Class 50 No. 50027 *Lion* reaches the top of the bank on 27th June 1980 with the 09.15 Penzance-Paddington.

CJM

Until March 1959 a station existed at Plympton, on the outskirts of Plymouth. When this view was taken on 1st October 1984 all that remained was the closed signal box, latterly used by track staff, and mounds of earth where the platforms once stood. No. 50005 *Collingwood* passes the former station site with the 10.10 Paignton-Plymouth.

CJM

Before the days of nameplates, No. 50030 approaches Plymouth North Road station with the 13.30 Paddington-Penzance on 18th September 1976. At this time the Class 50s were ousting the loved 'Western' Class 52s from the West of England main line.

Brian Morrison

The 09.40 Paddington-Penzance service of 4th September 1984 passes Keyham station headed by No. 50003 *Temeraire*. As with many of the smaller stations considerable rationalisation has taken place in recent years, with this once thriving station now only having two platforms and no goods yard.   *CJM*

To the west of Keyham station the railway crosses over an iron girder viaduct crossing Weston Lake Mill adjacent to the large MoD Navy establishment. Heading west on 20th June 1985 No. 50049 *Defiance* hauls the 13.30 Paddington-Penzance.   *CJM*

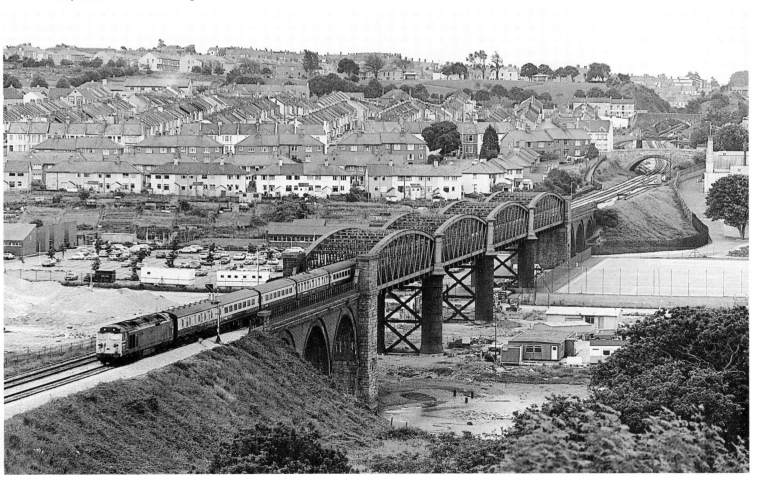

The eight mile Paignton branch from Newton Abbot has seen considerable Class 50 activity, especially on summer Saturdays with many additional holiday trains. On 1st July 1984 No. 50006 *Neptune* is seen near Torre with the 15.25 Paignton-Paddington.

CJM

During the late 1980s the Class 50s were diagrammed for a number of stone services operating over the former LSWR North Devon line to Meldon Quarry. On 8th May 1989, 'more yellow' No. 50016 *Barham* approaches Yeoford with a Meldon Quarry-Bristol ballast service. The Class 50 on this train would have operated throughout to Bristol, having to run-round at Exeter Riverside yard.

Reg Jones

During the summer of 1990, due to a shortage of suitable dmu stock, a Class 50 and stock was used on the Exeter-Barnstaple line on several days. On 26th July No. 50008 *Thunderer* arrives at Exeter with the 17.46 service from Barnstaple.

CJM

Slowly approaching the Cornish bank of the River Tamar, high above the Saltash roof tops, No. 50020 *Revenge* crosses the Royal Albert Bridge on 19th September 1976 with the 11.00 Plymouth-Penzance stopping service.

Brian Morrison

With the tail of the train passing over Coldrenic Viaduct, No. 50009 *Conqueror* heads the up "Cornishman" service from Penzance to Leeds on 20th June 1980. The Class 50 would be removed from this service at Plymouth and replaced by a Class 47.

CJM

No.50032 *Courageous* hurries downgrade towards Liskeard on 3rd May 1985 with an additional service from Plymouth to Penzance. The majority of main line services travelling west of Plymouth make Liskeard their first station stop. *CJM*

It is unfortunate to record that the Motorail service linking London and St Austell, formed of Motorail flat wagons no longer runs, and the few customers that require the Motorail service are directed to Paddington where their charges are loaded into vans. On 22nd June 1980 the St Austell-Kensington service hauled by No. 50012 *Benbow* passes over Bolitho Viaduct near Liskeard. *CJM*

Looking west from the overbridge at Liskeard station, showing how the platforms are slightly staggered, No. 50008 *Thunderer* arrives with a Mk 2 train formation on 25th June 1980 forming the 09.15 Penzance-Paddington. Although most of the BR network now has colour light signalling, Liskeard was still using semaphore signals at the end of 1990.

CJM

During the early 1980s, and even as late as 1987 many of the Cornish main line passenger services were loco-hauled, giving the chance for a Class 50 roster. On 17th June 1980 No. 50029 *Renown*, passes Cutmadoc, near Bodmin Road with the 09.15 Penzance-Paddington.

CJM

One of the most famous of the Cornish viaducts is Moorswater, located west of Liskeard, with its seven arches not only spanning the valley but also the clay line to the Moorswater ECC works. Heading west across the viaduct on 3rd May 1985 No. 50047 *Swiftsure* hauls the 15.00 Plymouth-Penzance.

CJM

As well as the passenger services in Cornwall, a sizeable amount of freight or departmental traffic is to be found. On 16th November 1987 green-liveried No. 50007 *Sir Edward Elgar* stands in the loop at Lostwithiel with an engineers' train bound for Truro, while dmmu set No. 955 passes by with ecs from Laira to St Ives.

Brian Morrison

By far the largest Railfreight customer in Cornwall is English China Clays (ECC) who have for many years transported clay and its allied products by rail. With a rake of the now obsolete 'clay hood' wagons No. 50043 *Eagle* departs from Lostwithiel on the Fowey branch with a train from St Blazey to Carne Point on 23rd April 1987.

Michael J. Collins

The Sunday 07.45 Kensington Olympia-St Austell passenger/Motorail service of 22nd June 1980 headed by No. 50012 *Benbow* passes Treesmill near Par.

CJM

From the same location as the previous illustration, but looking in the opposite direction, the 16.17 Penzance-Paddington of 1st April 1986 is lifted away from Par by No. 50005 *Collingwood*. In these lighting conditions the intensity of the headlight is quite apparent.

Michael J. Collins

Another of the Cornish locations that retained semaphore signalling throughout the 1980s was Par, where many photographers used these splendid structures to frame their pictures. No. 50041 *Bulwark* is seen approaching Par on 29th April 1985 with the 16.35 Plymouth-Penzance service formed of just five coaches.

CJM

With Par docks, used almost exclusively for the transport of china clay products on the horizon, Network SouthEast liveried No. 50018 *Resolution* hurries west with the daily Liverpool-Penzance service on 24th April 1987. *Michael J. Collins*

Mid-way between Par and St Austell is Carlyon Bay, where in addition to a pleasant beach there is a golf course providing some excellent views of the railway. No. 50003 *Temeraire* heads west on 3rd October 1984 with the 09.36 Liverpool-Penzance. *CJM*

Throughout the mid-1980s Class 50s were regularly deployed on local Cornish china clay duties, being normally 'based' at St Blazey. With just four clay slurry tanks in tow, No. 50043 *Eagle* heads west near Carlyon Bay on 22nd April 1987 with a trip to Blackpool driers, Burngullow. *Michael J. Collins*

Traffic levels in west Cornwall declined during the 1980s to an extent that the section of line between Burngullow and Probus was singled, the junction at the Burngullow end being opposite the ECC Blackpool clay driers. Standing next to the now rebuilt ECC driers complex on 22nd April 1987, No. 50047 *Swiftsure* pauses with a St Blazey-Burngullow 'Polybulk' working. *Michael J. Collins*

In the days when two tracks prevailed west of Burngullow, No. 50046 *Ajax* heads the 12.00 Penzance-Glasgow vans on 17th June 1980. The line diverging to the right behind the locomotive goes to the clay branches of Drinnick Mill and Parkandillack.

CJM

With Burngullow signal box on the right, and the massive clay drying towers of ECC Blackpool Works on the left, No. 50010 *Monarch* heads west with the 07.50 Bristol-Penzance on 3rd May 1985.

CJM

Some 21 months prior to its destructive derailment at Paddington, No. 50041 *Bulwark* is seen near St Austell on 22nd February 1982, at the head of an unfitted engineers' train bound for Truro yard.

Brian Morrison

One of the highlights of summer Saturdays in Cornwall during the late 1970s and early 1980s was the St Austell Motorail, which was often Class 50 powered. On 27th August 1982 No. 50003 *Temeraire* shunts the down service at St Austell. By the time this illustration was taken the service emanated from Paddington and not Kensington Olympia.

John Tuffs

On 9th June 1976, the then un-named No. 50015 passes Penwithers Junction, near Truro with the up "Cornish Riviera Express", the train in Cornwall being formed of only six coaches plus a van, the remainder of the eleven coach formation being attached at Plymouth. The single line diverging left at the rear of the train is the branch to Falmouth.
Brian Morrison

Although the majority of van trains have long been withdrawn from the timetable, a few still exist in Cornwall, linking Penzance with the main centres of Bristol, Birmingham and Glasgow. The 12.00 Penzance-Glasgow headed by No. 50006 *Neptune* passes Green Bottom near Chacewater on 1st May 1985.
CJM

One of the many redundant tin mines still to be found in the Duchy of Cornwall is seen on the left of this view taken at Scorrier near Redruth on 15th July 1977, showing No. 50002 heading the 10.05 Friday only Penzance-Sheffield.   *Brian Morrison*

Directly west of Hayle station is Hayle Viaduct, spanning both the River Hayle and the main A30 road. Crossing the viaduct on 2nd May 1985, No. 50001 *Dreadnought* heads a four coach 15.00 Plymouth-Penzance.   *CJM*

The first Class 50 to be withdrawn, No. 50011 *Centurion* in unrefurbished condition pulls around the tight curve at Marazion near Penzance on 23rd June 1980 with the daily Leeds-Penzance working. After its eventual withdrawal the nameplates were transferred to No. 50040.
CJM

In the course of their china clay duties the Class 50s have visited most yards and sidings in the Duchy, but the small, seldom used siding at Nanpean Wharf off the Parkandillack branch, is reported to have seen its first Class 50 on 24th April 1987, when this photograph was taken of No. 50047 *Swiftsure* with one empty bogie wagon.
Michael J. Collins

With a rake of CDA clay wagons behind, built during the mid-1980s at BREL Doncaster, and based on the successful mgr coal wagon, No. 50016 *Barham* passes Lanjeth on the Parkandillack branch with a St Blazey bound trip on 29th March 1988.

Michael J. Collins

The summer of 1987 was the last that loco-hauled passenger services were diagrammed for operation over the Par-Newquay line. On 15th August 1987 NSE liveried No. 50029 *Renown* winds around the curve near Roche with the 16.28 Newquay-Wolverhampton.

Brian Morrison

It is only in comparatively recent times that Class 50s have operated in any quantity in Wales, this dearth of Class 50 activity being attributable to the lack of Class 50 traction knowledge by South Wales based train crews. On 26th March 1987 No. 50003 *Temeraire* passes Gear Junction, west of Newport with the 12.10 Cardiff-Portsmouth Harbour duty.
CJM

A semi-regular Class 50 duty in South Wales from 1987 was at the head of the daily Swansea-Old Oak Common vans train. On 27th August 1987 the train passes Llanwern near Newport with No. 50033 *Glorious* providing the power.   *Michael J. Collins*

Although not actually in Wales, No. 50004 *St Vincent* heads downgrade at Pilning towards the Severn Tunnel on 11th July 1989 with a Gloucester-Cardiff air-braked freight.   *CJM*

Worcester Line

During the early 1980s many Paddington-Hereford, Worcester and Cotswold line services were taken over by Class 50s, providing some interesting photographic locations to capture the class. Approaching the fixed distant at Morton-in-Marsh on 19th April 1987, No. 50044 *Exeter* heads the diverted 09.10 Liverpool-Poole.

Brian Beer

It is always pleasing to see a matching train and stock formation, particularly when painted in NSE livery. This was certainly the case on 19th April 1987 when No. 50044 *Exeter* was captured on film at Finstock with the 09.40 Paddington-Worcester.

Brian Beer

No. 50037 *Illustrious* departs from Worcester Shrub Hill on 24th April 1982 at the head of the 16.03 service bound for Paddington.

Brian Beer

With yesterday's age of transport in the foreground – the narrow boat, Class 50, No. 50004 *St Vincent* crosses the River Avon near Evesham on 11th May 1982 while working the 16.03 Worcester-Paddington.

Brian Beer

Thankfully there have been few major accidents or derailments that have involved Class 50s. However like all types, mishaps do occur, often with, to say the least, interesting results. This is the sight that faced recovery crews at Lancaster on 14th March 1968 when No. D431 hauling a parcels train collided with buffer stops and appeared to start burrowing into the ground!

Brian Bell

On 29th January 1979, No. 50003 *Temeraire* was involved in a rear end collision with the up West of England sleeping car train at Plymouth. The result of the impact pushed the Class 50's No. 2 cab end in, and after removal to Laira depot an inspection was carried out and a repair contract placed with BREL Doncaster, where the locomotive is seen in 1980.

Jeremy de Souza

Serious front end damage was received by No. 50044 *Exeter* on 9th August 1982 whilst hauling empty stock at Malago Vale carriage sidings, Bristol. After recovery the locomotive was taken to BREL Doncaster for detailed inspection and repair.

CJM

On occasions shunting mishaps or collisions occur at maintenance depots. This was the case in April 1980 when No. 50038 *Formidable* suffered side swipe damage at Laira depot, the results of which are depicted. Repairs to this damage were rectified at Laira.

CJM

An interesting mishap to befall a Class 50 was on 5th April 1985 when No. 50004 *St Vincent* was hauling the 10.27 Paddington-Paignton. While departing from Westbury it was routed onto the up line in error, and before the driver could bring his charge to a stand the locomotive and first five coaches had passed through the pointwork. The illustration shows the scene after the coaches has been pushed back through the pointwork to regain the correct line. It was not possible for the locomotive to be recovered the same way, and it had to travel via the up line to Westbury. Thankfully no serious damage was caused to either locomotive, stock or passengers.

The first major derailment to occur to a Class 50 was on 23rd November 1983, when No. 50041 *Bulwark* derailed and turned onto its side outside Paddington station while hauling the "Night Riviera" service from Penzance. The damage was such that it took several days before rerailing was complete. However the locomotive was repaired by BREL Doncaster. Our picture shows the locomotive at Paddington after it was returned upright.

Barry Edwards

Above and right: One of the most serious acts of vandalism ever to occur on BR took place on the evening of 6th August 1989 when the 21.15 Oxford-Paddington was derailed at West Ealing by an article placed across the track. No. 50025 *Invincible* derailed and turned onto its side, and the remainder of the train was derailed. The upper illustration shows the locomotive on its side prior to recovery, while the picture right, shows the body mounted on a road low-loader awaiting departure from a supermarket car park to Old Oak Common depot.

Brian Morrison/Barry Edwards

Double Stamps

As mentioned previously, one of the most photographed sections of the WR main line is that along the Devon coast. It is pleasing to record that on a number of occasions double-heading of services takes place. On 19th April 1987 'more yellow' Nos 50008 *Thunderer* and 50031 *Hood* pull out of Kennerway Tunnel near Dawlish with ecs bound for Exeter.

CJM

216

It is very unlikely that any passenger service traversing the sea wall would require 5,400hp at the helm, and double-heading is usually employed to transfer additional locomotives to either Exeter or Plymouth. One service often double headed in 1988 was the 09.40 Plymouth-Portsmouth Harbour which conveyed additional traction to Exeter for engineers' duties. On 18th July 1988 the train is seen near Dawlish with NSE liveried Nos 50041 *Bulwark* and 50044 *Exeter* on the front. This picture is particularly pleasing as the entire train is finished in NSE colours.

217 *Reg Jones*

It is unusual to find Class 50s double-heading other classes of locomotive, as the Class 50s orange square multiple-control equipment is not compatible. On 18th July 1988 the 13.05 Truro-Ince & Elton company train is seen crossing Cockwood Harbour with train locomotive Class 47 No. 47654 *Finsbury Park* being operated in tandem with, Class 50 No. 50048 *Dauntless*.   *Reg Jones*

Due to its excessive weight, the 'Polybulk' train from Burngullow to Dover conveying export china clay is often double-headed over the Devon banks. On 2nd July 1987 the up service is seen along the sea wall with train engine Class 47 No. 47123 being assisted by Class 50 No. 50002 *Superb*.   *Reg Jones*

With early morning light giving almost perfect illumination, two Class 50s, both in NSE livery with No. 50030 *Repulse* leading, approach Langstone Rock, near Dawlish Warren on 23rd June 1989 with the 07.12 Newton Abbot-Exeter.

Reg Jones

On 24th May 1987 the 09.00 Oxford-Old Oak Common empty van service was unusually double-headed by Class 50 No. 50040 *Leviathan*, and Class 47 No. 47508 *SS Great Britain*. The reason for this tandem operation was the failure of the train locomotive. This illustration is taken at Southall.

Brian Morrison

50149

One of the biggest surprises in the Class 50 story came in August 1987 when No. 50049 *Defiance* was converted by Laira depot for Railfreight use, repainted in Railfreight triple grey livery and renumbered 50149. Sporting its cast Laira depot symbol on the cab side the locomotive is seen at Exeter stabling point on 14th November 1987 alongside NSE liveried No. 50017 *Royal Oak*.

CJM

After operating various trials for the Railfreight sector, principally on stone trains in the Westbury area, No. 50149 settled down to working china clay services in Cornwall. One duty that often took the locomotive away from the Duchy was the afternoon freight to Gloucester which the locomotive worked to Exeter. On 24th June 1988 No. 50149 crosses Cockwood Harbour with the 15.05 St Blazey-Gloucester freight.

CJM

With a rake of the new generation CDA clay wagons behind, No. 50149 passes the now closed Royal Albert Bridge signal box as it pulls off the bridge and into Devon with a trip from St Blazey to Tavistock Junction on 22nd June 1988.

CJM

Many of the larger modern air-braked wagon types are now used in the expanding china clay rail freight business, and for several years this has included the use of Traffic Services 'Polybulk' wagons. A short train of just four 'Polybulk' vehicles approaches St Austell on 30th June 1988 on a trip working from Burngullow to St Blazey headed by No. 50149. *CJM*

Although Railfreight were not totally happy with No. 50149's performance on general freight duties, the locomotive operated successfully in Cornwall, and was well liked by train crews. On 30th March 1988 the locomotive is seen passing Carlyon Bay with a trip from ECC Blackpool driers, Burngullow to St Blazey. *Michael J. Collins.*

Following the replacement of the time-honoured 'clay hoods' and the introduction of the new CDA wagons, train consists have been much shorter, as the capacity of the new wagons is considerably more. With a rake of 16 CDA wagons, No. 50149 departs from Lostwithiel bound for Carne Point. In the background Class 37 No. 37672 can be seen which had brought the train in from Burngullow.

Michael J. Collins

With a little effort some very pleasing pictorial views of Class 50s can be obtained in Cornwall. This pleasant view taken near Carne Point shows No. 50149 departing across the causeway with empty CDA wagons from the docks at Fowey bound for St Blazey on 30th March 1988.

Michael J. Collins

From the hills to the west of Lostwithiel a splendid view of trains leaving the station can be obtained. This illustration taken on 30th March 1988 shows No. 50149 *Defiance* taking the line to Carne Point with a rake of CDA wagons.

Michael J. Collins

During its short career No. 50149 is only reported to have operated two passenger duties, one being on 28th May 1988 when it piloted sister No. 50042 *Triumph* from Exeter to Paignton on the 13.05 service from Paddington. The train is seen departing from Dawlish.

CJM

Off the Beaten Track

Like all classes the 50s have had their regular stamping grounds, but on many occasions unusual routes and lines have been covered. On 20th March 1988 due to engineering work the 14.20 Exeter St Davids-Waterloo was diverted via Westbury, and is seen climbing Upton Scudamore bank with No. 50010 *Monarch* at the head.

Brian Beer

Another diversion on the Waterloo-Exeter line occurred on 3rd May 1987, when services were re-routed from Salisbury via the Wylye Valley to Westbury, Castle Cary and thence Yeovil. The 12.25 Exeter St Davids-Waterloo is seen with No. 50023 *Howe* in charge near the village of Heytesbury.

Brian Beer

Due to the main West of England line being blocked by engineering works at Taunton on 5th April 1986, services were routed via the Southern line to Yeovil and Yeovil Pen Mill to Castle Cary and the WR. The 08.15 Penzance-Paddington headed by No. 50044 *Exeter* pulls slowly into Yeovil Pen Mill. Note the old cattle pens in the left foreground.

Michael J. Collins

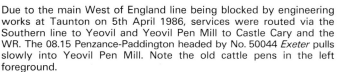

No. 50010 *Monarch* passes Purton, north of Lydney and skirts the bank of the River Severn on 3rd May 1987 while at the head of the 16.45 Cardiff-Birmingham New Street.

Brian Beer

Again with the River Severn in the background, a Class 50, No. 50008 *Thunderer* skirts its shores with the 16.45 Cardiff-Birmingham service of 19th April 1987. The train is formed of five Mk 1 carriages of which the second is a ScotRail example.

Brian Beer

Passing the little station of Freshford on the Avon Valley line, No. 50013 *Agincourt* heads a diverted 10.00 Plymouth-Paddington on 18th April 1981. The service was diverted via Hawkeridge Junction, Heywood Road Junction and the Berks & Hants line to reach Reading.

Brian Beer

Not only off the beaten track, but hauling a most unusual consist, No. 50044 *Exeter* heads the 09.10 Scunthorpe-Severn Tunnel Junction empty mgr train past Clay Cross Junction, south of Chesterfield on 31st August 1983. The locomotive was rostered for this train while returning to the WR after rectification work at BREL Doncaster Works.

John Tuffs

Following Class 50 overhauls at BREL Doncaster Works, the locomotives were handed back to the operators at Doncaster depot, from where they were returned to the WR by the most convenient means. This was sometimes the 09.43 Newcastle-Penzance, which on 29th May 1986 was headed by No. 50036 *Victorious* and photographed at Clay Mills near Burton.

John Tuffs.

During the mid-1980s the Class 50 diagrams were such that a locomotive was often 'spare' at Saltley, and if no LM traction was available this was sometimes 'borrowed' and used on the Lawley Street-Nottingham-Lawley Street Freightliner service. On 17th August 1984, No. 50003 *Temeraire* is seen between Clay Mills and Wetmore near Burton with the 15.21 Nottingham FLT to Lawley Street working.

John Tuffs

No. 50027 *Lion* was the 'borrowed' motive power on 4th July 1986 for the Freightliner working, and is seen passing the site of the former Branston station on the return run to Lawley Street.

John Tuffs

One of the early refurbished Class 50s, returned to the WR painted in original blue livery was No. 50047 *Swiftsure*. In this view the locomotive is seen returning to the WR following a casual repair at Doncaster Works at the head of the 14.28 York-Plymouth on 26th August 1983.

John Tuffs

The first time a Class 50 visited King's Cross was on 10th June 1977, when No. 50009 *Conquerer* hauled the 08.46 Hull-King's Cross and 14.10 King's Cross-Leeds. The locomotive was driven by a Doncaster-based crew who had been trained on the traction in readiness for Doncaster Works taking over repairs. This view shows the northbound service passing Stevenage.

David Percival

Following classified overhauls of Class 50s an active test run was always operated, originally this was to Newcastle, but in later years Peterborough was used as the termination point. On 23rd July 1985 No. 50040 *Leviathan* is seen at Werrington near Peterborough with a return Doncaster Works test special.
John Tuffs

On 12th June 1984 the usual motive power for the Peterborough-Cardiff vans train was not available and Class 50 No 50022 *Anson* was diagrammed for the service. The unusual motive power is seen departing from Peterborough.
John Rudd

Illustrations of two of the great English Electric designs together are not common, but this view taken at York on 7th March 1980 does just that. Class 55 'Deltic' No. 55019 *Royal Highland Fusilier* stands in the bay on a stopping service to King's Cross, while pulling away from the station, Class 50 No. 50002 *Superb* hauls the 09.50 Edinburgh-Plymouth, a service to which the Class 50 had been attached at York, following refurbishment at Doncaster.

Brian Beer

A route on the WR not usually associated with Class 50s is the Exmouth branch. However on rare occasions troop trains visit Lympstone and are sometimes headed by Class 50s. As no run-round provisions exist on the branch, trains are usually 'top and tailed'. On 4th August 1989 one such movement was operated with motive power being provided by No. 50020 *Revenge* on the Exmouth end, and Class 47 No. 47834 *Fire Fly* on the Exeter end. The train is seen near Polsloe Bridge.

CJM

Inclement Weather

Illustrations of trains operating in inclement weather always make pleasant pictures and are nice to look at, but for the photographer the story is somewhat different! On 8th February 1986 No. 50016 *Barham* passes Wellingborough in a snowstorm whilst in charge of the 'Derbyshire Dingle' railtour bound for Buxton.

Brian Beer

There are some years when it is very difficult to photograph a train in snow conditions in the south of the country, however a moderate fall was recorded on 15th January 1985 when No. 50045 *Achilles* was photographed passing Grateley in charge of the 13.10 Waterloo-Exeter St Davids service.

CJM

These two illustrations taken near Southampton on 19th January 1985 show Waterloo-Exeter St Davids route diversions. The view left depicts No. 50044 *Exeter* approaching Southampton with an up service, while the picture right, is of No. 50009 *Conqueror* departing from Southampton with the 10.38 from Waterloo.

Both Alex Dasi-Sutton

With a blanket of snow, and in somewhat dull conditions, No. 50027 *Lion* approaches the lower quadrant semaphore stop signal at Morton-in-Marsh on 8th March 1987 with the 09.40 (Sundays) Paddington-Worcester.

Brian Beer

Special Duties

Right: On a number of occasions Class 50s have been called upon to perform special duties, one such case was on 27th November 1986 when No. 50009 *Conqueror* was used on a track recording special to Weymouth. Included in the train formation was ex-GWR test car No. DW139 (at rear of train). This view of the train run was taken on Upway Bank near Weymouth.

Brian Beer

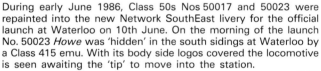

Facing page: Although not advertised, it is not uncommon to find nuclear flask traffic operating through the Devon countryside. On 22nd June 1989, green-liveried No. 50007 *Sir Edward Elgar* passes the site of the former Brent station with a Devonport Dockyard-Rosyth special.

Reg Jones

On 25th April 1988 a minor derailment occurred at Exeter Riverside Yard, and to re-rail the wagons the Laira allocated CM&EE crane was used. The service returning the crane from Exeter to Laira is seen pulling out of Clerk's Tunnel, Dawlish, motive power being provided by No. 50045 *Achilles*.

CJM

During early June 1986, Class 50s Nos 50017 and 50023 were repainted into the new Network SouthEast livery for the official launch at Waterloo on 10th June. On the morning of the launch No. 50023 *Howe* was 'hidden' in the south sidings at Waterloo by a Class 415 emu. With its body side logos covered the locomotive is seen awaiting the 'tip' to move into the station.

CJM

The Birmingham Road

The Paddington-Birmingham via High Wycombe line has seen some Class 50 activity in recent years. On 30th June 1987, No. 50013 *Agincourt* hammers through West Ruislip with the 17.53 Paddington-Banbury. On the right the LRT Central line tracks can be seen.

Brian Morrison

A new Saturday diagram from the introduction of the May 1989 timetable took a Class 50 to Wolverhampton on the 07.05 from Paddington. No. 50026 *Indomitable* is seen near Galton Junction, between Smethwick and Sandwell on 27th May 1989-the first occasion on which a Class 50 performed the duty. The locomotive returned to London with the 11.18 service from Wolverhampton.

Brian Beer

With a heavy exhaust plume, indicating that the locomotive is under full power, No. 50006 *Neptune* pulls away from Princes Risborough with the 06.22 Wolverhampton-Paddington on 13th August 1985.

Brian Beer

One of the most popular Class 50s has for some time been No. 50008 *Thunderer*, which is seen passing Loudwater near High Wycombe on 6th September 1985 at the head of the 06.22 Wolverhampton-Paddington.

John Stretton

Although displaying the Network SouthEast livery, and indeed hauling NSE liveried coaching stock, this night illustration of No. 50030 *Repulse* was taken at Birmingham New Street after arrival of a Paddington service. The train is preparing to depart empty for Oxley carriage sidings.

Mike Matthews

The popularity of the Class 50s has been demonstrated over the past years by the number of requests for railtour operation. One of the first tour organisers to favour Class 50 motive power was John Vaughan who requested several for his RPPR trips. On 12th August 1979 No. 50046 *Ajax* was used on "The Welsh Warrior" tour from London to the Welsh Valleys. The illustration shows the train at Oakdale.

CJM

On 26th February 1983, No. 50030 *Repulse* was the rostered motive power for the "Essex Explorer" tour which took a Class 50 to such diverse locations as Fenchurch Street, Tilbury and Shoeburyness. This view of the train was taken at Ripple Lane, Barking and because the train was running well over one hour late it was nearly dark. Note the "Hoover" headboard on the front.

Brian Morrison

The Hertfordshire Railtours "Derbyshire Dingle" operated on 8th February 1986 was powered by No. 50016 *Barham*, the tour commencing from Paddington with an eventual destination of Buxton. Part of the trip included traversing the Leicester-Burton freight line, and it is on this line at Gresley that we see the train.

John Tuffs

On 10th March 1984 a railtour entitled "Conway Crusader" was operated to North Wales, and such was the success of this trip that a re-run was arranged for 21st April. Motive power was provided by green-liveried No. 50007 *Sir Edward Elgar*, which was paired with Class 40 No. 40192 for part of its journey. The upper photograph shows the train with the Class 50 leading, west of Roman Bridge, while the lower illustration, taken at Llandudno Junction, shows the Class 40 leading the train off the single track Blaenau Ffestiniog branch.

Andrew Bannister/Larry Goddard

With the heads of 'gricers' peering from the windows, the SEG organised "Vulcan Van Train" of 15th March 1986 is seen powered by No. 50025 *Invincible* on the outskirts of Tunbridge Wells. One of the main operating problems of tours such as this is traction knowledge of the drivers, as on the SR no Eastern section drivers are trained on Class 50 operation, so pilot drivers have to be provided.
Alex Dasi-Sutton

There have been few Class 50s to operate passenger services through Leeds, however on 14th November 1987, No. 50020 *Revenge* was used on the "Skipton Skipper" tour organised by Pathfinder Tours. This nocturnal shot shows the locomotive under the overall roof, complete with a rake of Network SouthEast stock!
Peter Marsh

To mark the end of regular loco-hauled services on the Par-Newquay line a BR special was operated on Sunday 4th October 1987 between Paddington and Newquay, hauled throughout by Class 50s Nos 50036 *Victorious* and 50035 *Ark Royal*. The two Network liveried locomotives were well turned out by Old Oak Common and are seen passing Dawlish on the outward working.

CJM

Since their demise from the LM, the Class 50s have seldom been seen on Midland metals, but one such occasion was on 12th March 1988 when No. 50001 *Dreadnought,* in revised NSE livery, was used on the "Pennine 40 Farewell Railtour". The train is seen here devoid of any silly headboard near Queen's Park, passing Class 40 No. D200 and 'ETHEL 3' running light to the LM terminal to take over the next leg of the tour.

Brian Beer

With the crooked spire of Chesterfield church visible on the horizon, Class 50s Nos 50024 *Vanguard* and 50050 *Fearless* power the Pathfinder Tours "The Fellsman 2" past Hasland on 23rd April 1988.

John Tuffs.

Another illustration showing the spire of Chesterfield church is this of No. 50037 *Illustrious* heading the Pathfinder Tours "Yorkshire Venturer" of 7th August 1988. Often railtours are formed exclusively of NSE stock as tours emanate from the London area and these are the only spare sets of coaches available.

Peter Gater

No. 50035 *Ark Royal* in most unusual surroundings on 31st July 1988. It pulls into the restored station at Cranmore on the East Somerset Railway, having worked over the rarely used section between here and the Merehead Quarry Loop Junctions of Foster Yeoman. The train, a full rake of Network SouthEast stock, brought a party of members of the Permanent Way Institution from Guildford as part of their annual convention. Travel over the ESR itself was in another, steam hauled train which was the first ever 5-coach train run by the railway.

Peter Nicholson

Left: As far as photography is concerned the application of headboards on railtours looks messy, and many would prefer them not to be carried. Near the site of the closed Lea Bridge station on 3rd July 1988 "The Suffolkman" tour from Leicester to Ipswich winds around the curve at Temple Mills and past the closed Temple Mills West signal box headed by No. 50022 *Anson*.

Brian Morrison

BR Watford and Hertfordshire Railtours jointly operated "The Malt & Hops" tour of 29th October 1988 from Watford to Dover, Ramsgate, Kensington, Stratford, Ipswich and London King's Cross. Motive power was provided by Nos 50026 *Indomitable* and 50032 *Courageous*. This view shows the outward leg of the tour passing Acton Wells Junction.

Michael J. Collins

Above: It is sad to record that the withdrawal of the Class 50 fleet commenced in February 1987 when No. 50011 *Centurion* was taken out of service. By the end of 1990 almost half the fleet had been deleted from stock but at the time of writing it is envisaged that some examples will remain in traffic until 1992. After laying dumped at Laira for many months locomotives Nos 50012/14/22/47 were hauled away from Laira during March 1989, first to Exeter and then Taunton on their way to scrap dealer Vic Berry of Leicester. The upper view shows Nos 50047 and 50022 stabled at Exeter Riverside, while the middle picture shows Nos 50012 and 50014 in Taunton Fairwater Yard. Note the hole in the side of the latter where the number area had been cut away and sold. *Both Charles Woodland*

Devoid of its nameplate and minus much of its frontal equipment, No. 50013 stands at Old Oak Common on 24th November 1986. This locomotive was broken up by a private scrap dealer at Old Oak Common depot in June 1989. *CJM*

After their arrival at the scrapyard of V.Berry, Leicester the Class 50s did not remain intact for long. These two views taken on 7th May 1989 show No. 50022 *Anson* (above), and No. 50014 *Warspite* (below) in the advance stages of dismantling. *Both Chris Milner*

Overleaf: No. 50037 *Illustrious* passes Powderham in south Devon on 15th July 1983 at the head of the 10.20 Paddington-Penzance. *CJM*